ONE SKILLET

WQED
Multimedia
PITTSBURGH

A production of WQED Multimedia

ISBN 0-9769936-6-X

For other great merchandise, visit SHOP WQED at
www.wqed.org, or call 1-800-274-1307, or write to
SHOP WQED, 4802 Fifth Avenue, Pittsburgh, PA 15213

For WQED Multimedia:

Executive Vice President & General Manager
Deborah L. Acklin

Vice President, Business & Finance
Patty Walker

Director, Distribution & Client Services
Keyola Panza

Manager, Product Sales & Operations
Robyn Martin

Unit Manager
Janine Hovanec

America's Home Cooking Producer/Host
Chris Fennimore

Art Director
Dave Rohm

Cookbook Editor
Joyce DeFrancesco Carr

Table of Contents

Recipes were prepared on "America's Home Cooking: One Skillet"

Table of Contents

Recipes were prepared on "America's Home Cooking: One Skillet"

Table of Contents

* Recipes were prepared on "America's Home Cooking: One Skillet"

ONE SKILLET

Table of Contents

Recipes were prepared on "America's Home Cooking: One Skillet"

Beef, Veal and Lamb

Beef Skillet

DIRECTIONS

Cook beef until brown. Stir in boxed beans and rice, tomatoes, corn and water; bring mixture to a boil. Reduce heat, cover and simmer for 20 minutes. Serve with shredded cheese and/or sour cream.

INGREDIENTS

1 pound ground beef

1 (8-ounce) box black beans and rice

1 (28-ounce) can diced tomatoes

1 (10-ounce) bag frozen corn

2 1/2 cups water

1 cup shredded cheddar cheese (optional), for serving

1 cup sour cream (optional), for serving

SUBMITTED BY:
Joann Grosik, Mineral Point

California Skillet

DIRECTIONS

Heat oil in a large skillet and brown meat and onion. Drain fat. Add all remaining ingredients except cheese. Cover and simmer 20 to 30 minutes or until macaroni is tender. Uncover and sprinkle with cheese. Cover and heat until cheese melts. Makes 4 to 6 servings.

INGREDIENTS

1 tablespoon oil

1 pound lean ground beef

1 small onion, chopped

1 tablespoon chili powder

2 cups water

1 (10 3/4-ounce) can tomato soup

1 (12-ounce) can corn, undrained

1 tablespoon Worcestershire sauce

1 cup uncooked elbow macaroni

1/2 teaspoon salt

1/2 teaspoon pepper

1 cup shredded cheddar cheese

SUBMITTED BY:
Mary Keffalas, Butler

America's
HOME COOKING

9

Chili with Ground Beef and Macaroni

DIRECTIONS

In a 12-inch skillet, cook ground beef, onion and green pepper over high heat until all pan juices evaporate and meat is brown, stirring frequently. Stir in chili powder; cook 1 minute. Stir in tomatoes, macaroni, sugar, salt, crushed red pepper and water over high heat; bring to a boil. Reduce heat to low, cover and simmer 20 minutes or until macaroni is tender; stirring occasionally. Sprinkle cheese over mixture in skillet; cover and simmer until cheese melts, about 2 minutes. Serves 4 to 6.

INGREDIENTS

1 pound ground beef or ground turkey

1 medium onion, chopped

1 medium green pepper, cut into bite-size pieces

2 teaspoons chili powder, to taste

1 (14 1/2- to 16-ounce) can tomatoes, undrained

1 cup uncooked elbow macaroni

1 teaspoon sugar

1/2 teaspoon salt

1/4 teaspoon crushed red pepper (optional)

1 1/4 cups water

1/2 cup shredded muenster or monterey jack cheese

SUBMITTED BY:
Jody Clark Walter, Squirrel Hill

Cindy's Spicy Brisket

DIRECTIONS

Preheat oven to 375 degrees. Thoroughly defrost brisket and trim as much fat as possible. Sprinkle paprika, Creole seasoning, garlic salt, basil, rosemary and thyme over both sides of brisket; evenly covering it. Coat skillet with olive oil and sauté garlic and onion until soft. Add brisket to skillet and brown well on both sides. After meat is browned, add baby carrots. Mix french dressing, ketchup, mustard, teriyaki sauce, jam and wine together; add to skillet. Cover and bake for 1 hour; flip meat and add frozen veggies, filling the skillet. Cover, lower oven temperature to 325 degrees, and bake for 1 hour.

Remove meat from skillet and slice against grain into 1/4-inch-thick slices; return slices to skillet. Bake 30 minutes to 1 hour until tender. Serve with noodles and crusty bread. Serves 6.

INGREDIENTS

4 pounds brisket, trimmed

Paprika, to taste

Creole seasoning, to taste

Garlic salt, to taste

Basil, to taste

Rosemary, to taste

Thyme, to taste

Dash garlic-flavored olive oil

1 tablespoon minced garlic

1/2 large yellow onion, chopped

1 cup baby carrots

1/4 cup sweet and spicy french dressing

1/4 cup ketchup

2 tablespoons Dijon-style mustard

3 tablespoons teriyaki sauce

2 tablespoons apricot jam

Dash wine, any kind

1 (16-ounce) bag frozen veggies, preferably broccoli, beans or peas

SUBMITTED BY:
Cindy Minogue, O'Hara Township

Commish's Spanish Rice Dish

DIRECTIONS

In a bowl, mix hamburger and Worcestershire sauce (or cut flank steaks into strips and sauté in Worcestershire sauce). Cook at medium-high heat in a large, deep skillet. When fully cooked, set meat aside and reserve juices. Wipe skillet dry; reduce heat to medium. Place rice in dry skillet and stir constantly to release nutty, toasty flavor of rice. Add oil as rice begins to brown. Add onion and garlic (and pepper if desired). Cook mixture, stirring frequently, until onions are clear. Add chicken stock; heat to a simmer. Add tomatoes, bay leaves, oregano, salt and pepper. Cover and lower heat; cook for 15 to 20 minutes until rice is done. Return meat and juices to skillet and stir. (Add small amount of water if needed.) Remove bay leaves and serve.

INGREDIENTS

2 pounds hamburger or flank steak

3 tablespoons Worcestershire sauce

3 cups medium or long-grain white rice

1/4 cup olive oil

1 large sweet onion, finely chopped

2 cloves garlic, minced

1 large green pepper, chopped (optional)

4 cups chicken stock

2 cups diced tomatoes, fresh or canned

2 bay leaves

1 tablespoon oregano

Salt and pepper, to taste

SUBMITTED BY:
Jim Scahill, Armstrong County

Easy Beef Stroganoff

DIRECTIONS

Brown meat and onion; drain fat. Add soup and stir. Add sour cream and mushrooms. Simmer until cooked thoroughly. Season with salt and pepper. Serve over noodles or rice. Serves 4.

INGREDIENTS

1 1/2 pounds ground chuck or round steak

1 small to medium onion, chopped

1 (10 1/2-ounce) can cream of mushroom soup

1/2 pint sour cream

1 (4 1/2-ounce) jar sliced mushrooms

Salt and pepper, to taste

SUBMITTED BY:
Marilyn Smith, Bethel Park

America's
HOME COOKING

Famous Camp Stew

DIRECTIONS

Brown beef and onions; drain. Add peppers, potatoes and baked beans to skillet. Add water and mix well. Bring mixture to a simmer. Cover and cook until potatoes are tender, about 20 to 30 minutes. Add a little water as needed. Serve with a tossed salad and applesauce.

INGREDIENTS

1 pound lean ground beef

1 medium onion, chopped

1/2 green pepper, chopped

4 cups peeled and cubed white potatoes

2 (1-pound) can baked beans

1/2 cup water, or as needed

SUBMITTED BY:
Pat Prohaska, Bradenville

Ground Beef Soup

DIRECTIONS

Brown ground beef with onion; drain excess fat. Add vegetables, mushrooms and soup; stir. Add water and bring to a rapid boil; add soup noodles. Cook noodles according to package directions.

INGREDIENTS

1 pound ground beef

1 small onion, chopped

1 (14 1/2-ounce) can mixed vegetables

1 (3-ounce) can mushrooms

1 (14 1/2-ounce) can cream of tomato soup

3 (14 1/2-ounce) cans water

1 (12-ounce) package fine egg noodles

SUBMITTED BY:
Sally Kessler, Gibsonia

America's
HOME COOKING

Hamburger Mixture

DIRECTIONS

Coat a large skillet with cooking spray. Sauté ground beef, celery and onion until beef is brown and celery and onion are transparent. Drain beef mixture in colander to remove excess oil. Return mixture to skillet and slowly add 1 packet of brown gravy and 1 cup of water. Simmer and stir. Repeat with remaining brown gravy and water, stirring until thick. Serve over mashed potatoes, rice or egg noodles.

INGREDIENTS

Nonstick cooking spray

1 pound ground beef

1 stalk celery, chopped

1 small onion, chopped

3 (3/4-ounce) packets brown gravy mix

3 cups water

SUBMITTED BY:
Linda Heil, Pittsburgh

16

Hearty Skillet Stew for Two

DIRECTIONS

In a large nonstick skillet coated with cooking spray, brown steak with onion. Stir in cabbage, carrots, potato, water, soy sauce and sugar; bring to a boil. Reduce heat, cover and simmer for 25 minutes or until carrots, cabbage and potato are tender. In a small bowl, combine cornstarch and cold water until smooth; stir in beef mixture. Bring to a boil; cook and stir for 1 to 2 minutes or until thickened. Serves 2.

INGREDIENTS

Nonstick cooking spray

1/2 pound boneless beef top round steak, cut into 1/2-inch cubes

1/3 cup chopped onion

2 cups chopped cabbage

2 medium carrots, chopped

1 medium potato, cut into 1/2-inch chunks

3/4 cup water

1/3 cup reduced-sodium soy sauce

2 to 3 tablespoons sugar

1/2 teaspoon cornstarch

1 teaspoon cold water

SUBMITTED BY:
Lois Richardson, Springdale

America's
HOME COOKING

17

Hot Dogs in Hot Beans

DIRECTIONS

Mix beans and salsa in a large, deep skillet. Add honey mustard, brown sugar, garlic and onion; mix well. Simmer until mixture is hot and boiling. (If serving hot dogs on buns, leave whole.) Cut hot dogs into penny rounds and place in hot bean mixture; cover. Simmer for 10 to 15 minutes, stirring occasionally. Serve in bowls (or, if whole, on hot dog buns with bean mixture on top). Top with condiments or cheddar cheese.

INGREDIENTS

1 (16-ounce) can baked beans with onions

1 (16-ounce) can chili kidney beans, hot

1 (16-ounce) jar medium salsa

2 tablespoons honey mustard

2 tablespoons brown sugar

1 tablespoon minced garlic

1 large sweet onion, diced

1 pound hot dogs

Buns, for serving (optional)

Shredded cheddar cheese (optional)

SUBMITTED BY:
Monica Narr, Crafton

Meal-in-One Casserole

DIRECTIONS

Preheat oven to 375 degrees. In a skillet over medium heat, cook beef until no longer pink; drain. Put potatoes in greased 2-quart baking dish. Top with beef and onion. Place peas in the center of the baking dish and arrange mushrooms around them. Sprinkle with salt, pepper and sesame seeds. Drizzle with butter. Cover and bake for 50 to 60 minutes.

INGREDIENTS

1 pound ground meat

3 medium unpeeled potatoes, thinly sliced

1 medium onion, sliced and separated into rings

1 cup peas

1 1/2 cups sliced mushrooms

1 1/2 teaspoon salt

1/4 teaspoon pepper

1 teaspoon sesame seeds

3 tablespoons butter, melted

SUBMITTED BY:
Betty Pandullo, Blairsville

America's
HOME COOKING

Mom's One-Pot Seven-Bone Roast with Potatoes and Carrots

DIRECTIONS

Season roast with salt and pepper (or other favorite seasonings). In a large skillet, sear roast in oil until browned. Add enough soup or consommé to cover roast; add onion and bring to a boil. Cover roast, lower heat to simmer and cook for 1 1/2 to 2 hours. Occasionally, check the rate of evaporation of the soup or consommé. If necessary, add another can of soup or consommé to keep the roast covered and moist. After 1 1/2 to 2 hours, add potatoes and carrots. Cover and continue to simmer for 30 minutes.

NOTE

The soup or consommé with sliced onions makes a delicious gravy.

INGREDIENTS

1 7-bone roast

Salt and pepper, to taste

Cooking oil

2 to 3 (10 1/2-ounce) cans onion soup or beef consommé

1 large onion, diced

4 whole potatoes, peeled and quartered

4 whole carrots, peeled and cut into large pieces

SUBMITTED BY:
Paul Fronczek, Pittsburgh

20

Nacho Joes

DIRECTIONS

In a large skillet, heat oil and cook onion and green pepper. Add ground chuck, season with salt and pepper, and brown well. Add taco seasoning, garlic and Worcestershire sauce; simmer. Add chile con queso and simmer on low for 15 minutes.

To serve, place mixture on buns and eat like traditional sloppy joes with tortilla chips on the side or place tortilla chips on a dish and top with nacho meat mixture, jalapenos, sour cream and additional shredded cheese or salsa, if desired.

NOTE

This mixture may also be used to top baked potatoes, pasta or french fries for a delicious side dish or meal.

INGREDIENTS

2 tablespoons oil

1 red onion, diced

1 green pepper, diced

1 pound ground chuck

Salt and pepper, to taste

1 (1 1/4-ounce) envelope taco seasoning mix

2 tablespoons minced garlic

2 teaspoons Worcestershire sauce

1 (16-ounce) jar medium chile con queso

Buns, for serving

Tortilla chips, for serving

Sour cream (optional)

Jalapeno peppers (optional)

Salsa (optional)

Shredded cheese (optional)

SUBMITTED BY:
Monica Narr, Crafton

Not-So-Sloppy Sloppy Joes

DIRECTIONS

Sauté onion in water till golden; remove from pan. Sauté beef until fully cooked; drain any grease or excess liquid. Return onions to pan, add seasoning and mix well. Add soup, mix well again and heat through. Serve on kaiser or onion rolls with coleslaw on the side.

INGREDIENTS

1 medium onion, chopped

1 1/2 pounds ground beef

Salt and pepper, to taste

Garlic powder, to taste

Worcestershire sauce, to taste

1 (10 3/4-ounce) can cream of mushroom soup

Kaiser or onion rolls, for serving

SUBMITTED BY:
Connie Bokras, Johnstown

One-Dish Veal Cutlet with Vegetables

DIRECTIONS

Preheat oven to 350 degrees. Season cutlets with salt and pepper. Heat olive oil in deep frying pan and add cutlets. Brown cutlets; transfer to baking pan. Add tomato puree, garlic and chicken broth. Season vegetables with salt and pepper and layer with lemon slices over cutlets Dot with butter and some additional olive oil, adding herb sprigs if desired. Bake for 55 minutes.

INGREDIENTS

Salt and pepper, to taste

2 to 3 veal cutlets

3 tablespoons olive oil

1/2 cup tomato puree

1/2 teaspoon minced garlic

1/2 cup chicken broth

2 potatoes, peeled and sliced into rounds

1 onion, peeled and sliced into rounds

1 tomato, sliced into rounds

1 zucchini, sliced lengthwise

1 lemon, sliced into rounds

1/4 cup (1/2 stick) butter

2 sprigs each parsley, thyme and rosemary (optional)

SUBMITTED BY:
Harriet Matthews, Canonsburg

America's
HOME COOKING

One-Pot Salsa Beef Skillet

DIRECTIONS

Brown ground beef in skillet; drain and return to skillet. Stir in water, salsa and macaroni. Bring to a boil, reduce heat to low and cover. Simmer 10 minutes or until macaroni is tender, stirring twice. Add corn and cheese sauce mix; cook 2 minutes, or until heated through, and blend well. Ladle into dish and sprinkle with shredded cheese and green onion. Serves 4 to 6.

INGREDIENTS

1 pound lean ground beef

2 cups water

1 cup thick and chunky salsa

1 (14-ounce) package deluxe macaroni and cheese dinner

2 cups frozen corn

1/2 cup shredded Mexican-style cheese, for garnishing

1 green onion, chopped, for garnishing

SUBMITTED BY:
Lois Richardson, Springdale

One-Skillet Gyro Spectacular

Directions

In a large skillet, over medium heat, sauté ground lamb with garlic and salt and pepper. Cook for 15 minutes until medium brown and done to taste; drain fat. Add red and green pepper, mushrooms and onions. Cover and simmer for 10 minutes. Serve in pita bread with sour cream, ranch dressing, cucumber and tomato slices, and lettuce leaves.

Ingredients

1 pound ground lamb

1 tablespoon minced garlic

1 teaspoon salt

Fresh ground pepper, to taste

1 cup sliced red and green peppers

1 cup fresh sliced mushrooms

2 medium yellow onions, sliced

1 (12-ounce) package pita bread, for serving

Sour cream, for serving

Ranch dressing, for serving

Cucumber, sliced, for serving

Tomato, sliced, for serving

Lettuce leaves, for serving

SUBMITTED BY:
Eddie Grimes, Greentree

Oriental Steak in Orange Sauce

DIRECTIONS

Heat oil in 12-inch skillet until hot. Whisk beef broth and orange juice together; set aside. Stir-fry scallions for 1 minute. Add beef and stir-fry for 3 minutes. Add vegetables and mushrooms and stir-fry for 3 minutes. Add broth and orange juice, soy sauce, brown sugar, and grated orange rind. Mix in uncooked rice, cover and simmer 2 minutes. Turn off heat and let stand for 3 minutes. Top with red and green peppers.

INGREDIENTS

1/4 cup vegetable oil

1/2 cup beef broth

3 tablespoons orange juice

3 scallions, chopped

1 (12-ounce) flank or minute steak, cut crosswise into 1/2-inch strips

1 (10-ounce) bag frozen Chinese vegetables, thawed and drained

1 cup thinly sliced mushrooms

1 tablespoon soy sauce

2 tablespoons brown sugar

1 teaspoon grated orange rind

1 cup uncooked quick-cooking rice

1/2 cup each sliced red and green pepper

SUBMITTED BY:
Sandra Adams, Pittsburgh

Pepper Steak

DIRECTIONS

Mix first 9 ingredients. Marinate steak in mixture for at least 1 hour or up to 6 hours. Heat a heavy skillet or wok until very hot. Remove steak from marinade, reserving liquid. Place peanut or vegetable oil in skillet, add steak and stir-fry until just browned on all sides. Remove steak to a warm plate. Sauté peppers and onion in the same skillet until onions begin to brown. Return steak to skillet, add reserved marinade and beef stock, and cook until peppers begin to soften. Serve over rice.

INGREDIENTS

1/4 cup soy sauce

1 tablespoon chopped ginger

2 tablespoons sherry, vermouth or white wine

1 teaspoon sesame oil

1 teaspoon Worcestershire sauce

1/2 teaspoon hot sauce

1/2 teaspoon rice wine vinegar

1 tablespoon minced garlic

1 tablespoon cornstarch

1 pound pepper steak (or any beef sliced thinly across grain)

1 to 2 tablespoons peanut or vegetable oil

1 cup seeded and sliced assorted sweet peppers

1 medium onion, sliced

1/4 to 1/2 cup beef stock

SUBMITTED BY:
Jim Baran, Pittsburgh

Pressure Cooker Beef with Red Wine

DIRECTIONS

Place pressure cooker over medium-high heat. Add 1 tablespoon olive oil. Season beef cubes with salt, pepper and 1/4 teaspoon thyme. Sauté in pressure cooker until browned on all sides; remove beef to a warm plate.

Add 1 tablespoon olive oil, mushrooms, onions, salt and pepper, and 1/4 teaspoon thyme to pressure cooker. Sauté until mushrooms and onions are golden. Add beef, wine, potatoes, bay leaves, salt, pepper and 1/2 teaspoon thyme. Secure lid and, following pressure cooker's directions, cook for 15 minutes. After opening lid, remove bay leaves and adjust seasonings. Add potato starch mixture and stir to thicken sauce.

NOTE

This recipe can also be made in a heavy pan, such as a Dutch oven. Cover and cook over medium-low heat for 45 to 60 minutes.

INGREDIENTS

2 tablespoons olive oil, divided

1 teaspoon dried thyme

1 pound cubed beef

Salt and pepper, to taste

1 teaspoon thyme, divided

1/2 pound white mushrooms, quartered

1/2 pound pearl onions

3/4 bottle hearty red wine

1 pound small white potatoes, halved

2 bay leaves

1 tablespoon potato starch dissolved in 1 tablespoon water

SUBMITTED BY:
Jim Baran, Pittsburgh

Prune Juice Roast

DIRECTIONS

Combine first 4 ingredients in skillet, add roast and spoon mixture over it. Cover and simmer about 2 1/2 to 3 hours or until meat is tender. Chill overnight in refrigerator.

The next day, remove all the fat from roast. Boil new potatoes and carrots until tender. Place roast in skillet; add beets while it reheats. Add peas to skillet at the last moment to prevent overcooking and loss of color. Serve roast and vegetables with juice on the side.

OPTION

Combine liquid from beets and pan juices. Dissolve 1 tablespoon cornstarch in 1/2 cup prune juice and add to hot mixture, spoon over meat and vegetables.

NOTE

This is also an excellent recipe for beef short ribs.

INGREDIENTS

1 1/2 cups prune juice

1 medium onion

1 tablespoon vinegar

1/4 cup soy sauce

1 (1 3/4-pound) beef roast (chuck, sirloin tip, blade, etc.)

6 to 8 new potatoes

4 carrots, peeled and chopped

1 (14 1/2-ounce) can drained beets, sliced or whole

3/4 cup green peas

SUBMITTED BY:
Ralph Peabody, Cranberry Township

America's
HOME COOKING

Ranch Supper

DIRECTIONS

Fry chopped bacon in large skillet; pour off all but 2 tablespoons grease. Crumble raw ground beef over bacon. Add salt and pepper. Add onion, potatoes, vegetables, and salt and pepper in layers over ground beef and bacon. Cover and cook over low heat for approximately 35 minutes or until done, stirring occasionally. Serve with hot garlic bread and salad, if desired.

INGREDIENTS

3 slices bacon, chopped

1 pound ground beef

Salt and pepper, to taste

1 large onion, sliced thin

2 large or 3 medium potatoes, sliced thin

1 (10-ounce) box frozen cauliflower

1 (10-ounce) box frozen corn or lima beans

1 (10-ounce) box frozen brussels sprouts

1 small head red cabbage, cut into 3 or 4 wedges

SUBMITTED BY:
JoAnn Hilliard, East Liverpool

Reuben Pie

DIRECTIONS

Preheat oven to 400 degrees. Bake pie shell about 6 minutes. Combine breadcrumbs, milk, onion, egg, mustard, salt and pepper in a large bowl. Add corned beef, sauerkraut and ground beef. Layer meat mixture and cheese in pie shell, ending with cheese. Bake for 35 to 40 minutes. Add topping (mix sour cream and horseradish) to pie after baking, if desired.

INGREDIENTS

1 (9-inch) deep-dish pie shell

3/4 cup rye or white bread crumbs

1/3 cup evaporated milk

1 small onion, chopped

1 egg, beaten

1/2 teaspoon mustard

1/4 teaspoon salt

Dash pepper

1 (12-ounce) can corn beef

1 (8-ounce) can sauerkraut, drained

1/2 pound ground beef

4 ounces Swiss cheese, sliced

TOPPING (OPTIONAL):

1 cup sour cream

1 tablespoon horseradish

SUBMITTED BY:

JoAnn Hilliard, East Liverpool

Russian Cabbage

DIRECTIONS

Sauté ground meat, onion, garlic, and salt and pepper until meat loses its color. Add cabbage; mix. Squeeze tomatoes over top of cabbage and stir. Cook until tender and cabbage takes on a pink tinge.

INGREDIENTS

1 pound ground meat

1 medium onion, chopped

2 cloves garlic, chopped

Salt and pepper, to taste

1 (3-pound) cabbage head, quartered, cored and sliced

2 tomatoes

SUBMITTED BY:
Father Joseph Rabickon, Apollo

Simple Simon Skillet Pie

DIRECTIONS

In a skillet, stir flour into tomatoes and olives. Bring to a boil, stirring constantly. Add frankfurters. Cut biscuits into quarters and place on top of tomato mixture. Sprinkle with cheese. Cover and simmer gently for 30 minutes.

INGREDIENTS

1/4 cup flour

2 (16-ounce) cans seasoned stewed tomatoes

1/2 cup pitted sliced black olives

8 frankfurters, cut in half lengthwise

1 (12-ounce) can refrigerated biscuits

1 cup shredded cheddar cheese

SUBMITTED BY:
Theresa Gawryk, Pittsburgh

America's
HOME COOKING

Skillet Reubens

DIRECTIONS

Scrub potatoes, leaving skins on. Using a food processor, mandolin or sharp knife, slice the potatoes about 1/4 inch thick. In a large nonstick skillet, melt butter over medium heat. Place the potatoes in a skillet, starting in the center and working out in a circle, overlapping potatoes to cover the bottom of the skillet and halfway up the sides. Toss the onions on the potatoes and season with salt and pepper. Cover skillet and reduce heat to medium-low; cook for 20 minutes or until potatoes are tender and cooked through. (They should be nicely browned on the bottom.) Pour dressing over potatoes then layer corned beef, sauerkraut and cheese. Cook 10 to 15 minutes over medium-low heat until heated through and cheese is melted.

INGREDIENTS

4 medium red-skinned potatoes

1 tablespoon butter or margarine

1/2 small onion, chopped

1/4 teaspoon salt

1/4 teaspoon pepper

1/2 (16-ounce) bottle Thousand Island dressing

4 to 6 ounces deli corned beef, chopped

1/2 (16-ounce) can Bavarian-style sauerkraut

6 ounces Swiss cheese, shredded

SUBMITTED BY:
Kimberlee Love, North Side

34

Sloppy Joes

DIRECTIONS

In a large skillet, brown meat and onions until brown. Add mustard, ketchup and soup. Let simmer for several minutes. Heat, grill or toast buns or rolls. Serves 8 to 10.

INGREDIENTS

1 1/2 pounds lean ground meat

1 small sweet onion, chopped or diced

1 tablespoon yellow or hot mustard

1/4 cup ketchup

1 (10 3/4-ounce) can chicken gumbo soup

Buns or hard rolls, for serving

SUBMITTED BY:
Diana Sorg, Trafford

America's
HOME COOKING

Spanish Noodles

Directions

Fry bacon in a skillet and sear the ground meat quickly. Without stirring, add the noodles, tomatoes, chili sauce, green pepper, onion, salt and pepper in layers. Lower heat and cook for 30 minutes covered.

Ingredients

2 pieces bacon, cut in 1-inch pieces

1 pound ground meat

1 (12-ounce) bag egg noodles, uncooked

3 cups tomatoes plus 1/2 cup water

1/2 cup chili sauce

1/2 green pepper, diced

1 onion, diced

Salt and pepper, to taste

Submitted by:
Carole Ladik, Pittsburgh

Spanish Rice Dinner

DIRECTIONS

Mix all ingredients together and cook in skillet on stove top or in a 350-degree oven for 30 minutes. If mixture is too dry, add 1 or 2 cans of tomato sauce while cooking.

INGREDIENTS

1 pound ground meat

1 (14 1/2-ounce) can stewed tomatoes

1 (8-ounce) can cut green beans (can use waxed or frozen beans if desired)

1/2 to 3/4 cup uncooked rice

1 tablespoon sugar

1 teaspoon salt or garlic salt

1/4 teaspoon black pepper

1 teaspoon Worcestershire sauce

1 to 2 (8-ounce) cans tomato sauce (optional)

SUBMITTED BY:
A Friend of Public Television

America's
HOME COOKING

Spicy Beef Zucchini Skillet

DIRECTIONS

In a large skillet, brown beef; drain fat. Add oil, zucchini, onion and garlic to beef and cook for 2 minutes. Season mixture and stir. Add picante sauce; cook and stir for 5 minutes or until vegetables are crisp-tender. Add tomato; cook for 2 minutes or until heated through. Remove from heat and sprinkle with cheese. Serves 4.

INGREDIENTS

3/4 pound ground beef

2 tablespoons vegetable oil

4 cups chopped zucchini

1 cup chopped onion

2 garlic cloves, minced

1/2 teaspoon crushed red pepper

1/4 teaspoon dried oregano

1/2 teaspoon Italian seasoning

1/4 teaspoon salt

2/3 cup picante sauce

1 large tomato, peeled, seeded and chopped

1/2 cup shredded monterey jack cheese

SUBMITTED BY:
Donna Sunderlin, DuBois

Steak Pizzaiola

DIRECTIONS

Heat the oil in a large skillet over high heat. Add the steak and brown well on both sides. Remove steak from the pan and reduce heat to medium. Add the onion and garlic and cook for about 1 minute. Add the hot cherry peppers, if desired, and tomato paste. Roughly chop or squeeze the tomatoes and add to pan along with the spices. Bring to a boil then cover and lower to a simmer. Cook for 1 1/2 hours until extremely tender.

INGREDIENTS

1 tablespoon olive oil

1 (3-pound) chuck steak

1 large onion, sliced

2 cloves garlic, peeled

Hot cherry peppers (optional)

2 tablespoons tomato paste

1 (28-ounce) can peeled plum tomatoes

1 bay leaf

1 teaspoon oregano

1 teaspoon salt

1 teaspoon dried basil

Pepper, to taste

SUBMITTED BY:
Chris Fennimore, Pittsburgh

America's
HOME COOKING

Taco One-Skillet Meal

DIRECTIONS

Cook ground beef and onions together until meat is no longer pink. Drain fat. Drain tomatoes and reserve juice. Add enough water to juice to make 2 1/2 cups liquid; pour in pan. Add tomatoes, rice and taco seasoning; stir. Bring to a boil, cover and reduce heat to simmer until all liquid is absorbed, about 25 minutes. Sprinkle each serving with cheese and place lettuce on top. Serves 4.

INGREDIENTS

1 pound ground beef

1 large onion, diced

1 (16-ounce) can diced tomatoes

Water

1 cup uncooked long-grain rice

1 (1 1/4-ounce) package taco seasoning

1 cup shredded cheddar cheese, for serving

2 cups shredded lettuce, for serving

SUBMITTED BY:
Amanda Hudson, Hopewell

Veal di Napoli

DIRECTIONS

Pound cutlets 1/4 inch thick and then cut into serving size pieces. In a large skillet, brown meat quickly in hot oil; season with salt. In same skillet, combine tomatoes, sauce mix and sherry. Heat to boiling, cover and simmer 10 minutes, stirring occasionally. Add onions, mushrooms with reserved liquid, and peas and carrots. Garnish with parsley if desired.

INGREDIENTS

1 1/2 pounds veal cutlets

2 tablespoons vegetable oil

1 teaspoon salt

1 (16-ounce) can tomatoes

1 (1 1/2-ounce) package spaghetti sauce mix with mushrooms

1/3 cup sherry

1 (16-ounce) can whole onions, drained

1 (6-ounce) can sliced mushrooms, drain and reserve liquid, adding water to equal 1 cup

1 (16-ounce) can peas and carrots, drained

Parsley, for garnishing

SUBMITTED BY:
Theresa Gawryk, Pittsburgh

America's
HOME COOKING

41

Western Skillet

DIRECTIONS

In a large skillet, cook beef over medium heat until no longer pink; drain. Stir in water, rice, peas, green beans, corn and soup mix; bring to a boil. Reduce heat; cover and simmer for 25 minutes or until rice is tender. Sprinkle with cheese. Serve with salad and toasted bread. Serves 4 to 6.

INGREDIENTS

1 pound ground beef

3 cups water

1 (14 1/2-ounce) can stewed tomatoes

1 1/2 cups uncooked long-grain rice

1/2 cup frozen peas, thawed

1/2 cup frozen green beans, thawed

1/3 cup frozen corn, thawed

1 (1 1/4-ounce) envelope onion soup mix

1 cup shredded cheddar or Swiss cheese

SUBMITTED BY:
Lois Richardson, Springdale

Pork, Ham and Sausage

Bavarian Sausage Skillet Supper

Directions

In a skillet, sauté coleslaw mix and carrots in butter until crisp-tender. Add water; bring to a boil. Stir in kielbasa and noodle mix. Return to a boil; cook 8 minutes or until noodles are done. Stir occasionally. Serves 5.

Ingredients

2 cups coleslaw mix

1 cup thinly sliced carrots

2 tablespoons butter

2 1/4 cups water

3/4 pound fully cooked kielbasa, sliced

1 (4 1/2-ounce) package quick-cooking noodles and sour cream sauce, mixed together

Submitted by:
Donna Sunderlin, DuBois

Breakfast Pizza

DIRECTIONS

Grease a 12-inch skillet. Prepare pizza crust according to package directions. Line bottom and sides (up to 1/2 inch high) of the skillet with dough. Beat eggs, milk, mustard and pepper in a medium bowl. Slowly pour egg mixture over crust. Sprinkle bacon and cheeses evenly over the eggs. Cover and cook over medium heat for 15 minutes or until crust is brown on the bottom. Slide out onto cutting board and slice into wedges.

INGREDIENTS

1 (6 1/2-ounce) package pizza crust mix

6 eggs

1/4 cup skim milk

1 tablespoon dark brown mustard

Dash pepper

6 slices bacon, cooked and crumbled

1/2 cup shredded cheddar cheese

1/2 cup shredded mozzarella cheese

SUBMITTED BY:
Marianne Keane, Glenfield

America's
HOME COOKING

Cajun Hot Stuff Pepper Pot

DIRECTIONS

In a large, deep skillet, heat oil, season hot sausage with salt and pepper, and brown well. Add onion, peppers, garlic and pepper flakes; mix well. Sauté until onions are translucent. Add Bloody Mary mix and stir. Bring to a boil; add rice. Cover, remove from heat and let sit for 5 to10 minutes.

INGREDIENTS

4 tablespoons oil

1 pound bulk hot sausage

Salt and pepper, to taste

1 large onion, diced

1 red bell pepper, diced

1 green bell pepper, diced

2 tablespoons minced garlic

1/2 teaspoon red pepper flakes

3 cups Bloody Mary mix

1 1/2 cups instant rice

SUBMITTED BY:
Heidi and Monica Narr, Crafton

Commish's Huntin' Western Omelet

DIRECTIONS

Heat a 12-inch deep skillet on medium-high heat; add oil. Add ham and stir. After 3 minutes, add pepper, onion, mushrooms, garlic and salt and pepper to taste. While simmering, crack eggs into bowl and mix in milk. Evenly pour egg mixture into skillet. Cover completely with cheese slices. Once omelet begins bubbling, turn it. Add drops of Worcestershire and hot sauces after turning omelet. Continue turning and flattening omelet until it becomes firm. Serves 6 or more.

INGREDIENTS

2 tablespoons olive oil

1 1/2 pounds ham, cubed into 1/4-inch pieces

1 large green pepper, chopped

1 large onion, chopped

8 ounces mushrooms, sliced

1 clove garlic, minced

Salt and pepper, to taste

1 dozen eggs

1 cup milk

1/2 pound American cheese, sliced

2 tablespoons butter

Dash Worcestershire sauce

Dash hot sauce

SUBMITTED BY:
Jim Scahill, Armstrong County

Commish's Skillet Aloha Dish

DIRECTIONS

Cut pork into 1/2-inch chunks. Drain pineapple, reserving juice in a bowl. Add soy sauce, nutmeg, cinnamon and black pepper to pineapple juice. Put cornstarch in a bag, add pork pieces, and shake to evenly coat them. In a deep 12-inch skillet, warm both oils until hot. Add ginger and garlic and stir-fry for 2 minutes. Add pork and cook until well browned, about 5 to 6 minutes. Add peppers, scallions and pineapple/soy sauce mixture. Increase heat to medium-high and bring to a boil. Stir until sauce thickens. Add pineapple chunks and cook 2 minutes. Serve immediately. Serves 6 to 7.

INGREDIENTS

1 (2-pound) boneless pork loin

1 (12-ounce) can pineapple chunks (or fresh)

1/2 cup soy sauce

1 teaspoon nutmeg

1 teaspoon cinnamon

Black pepper, to taste

2 tablespoons cornstarch

3 tablespoons olive oil

3 tablespoons sesame oil

4 large pieces fresh ginger, sliced

2 cloves garlic, minced

1 each large green and red bell pepper, chopped

4 scallions, chopped

SUBMITTED BY:
Jim Scahill, Armstrong County

Cynthia's First Date Chops

DIRECTIONS

Place chops on a tray and season all sides with bay seasoning and basil. Cover tray and let chops marinate for at least 1 hour or overnight.

Preheat oven to 350 degrees. Remove chops from tray and place in a pan. Bake for 30 minutes. Mix oil and sugar with onions, shallots and garlic. Remove pan from the oven and cover chops with the onion mixture and fruit cocktail. Return chops to oven and bake another 30 minutes. Serve immediately.

INGREDIENTS

4 center-cut pork chops

1 teaspoon bay seasoning

1 teaspoon basil

1/3 cup olive oil or butter

1 teaspoon sugar or sugar substitute

1/2 cup chopped red onions

2 small shallots, chopped

1/4 cup chopped elephant garlic

1 (8 1/4-ounce) can fruit cocktail

SUBMITTED BY:
Cynthia Hill, Duquesne

America's
HOME COOKING

Dave's T&B (Turn and Burn) Jambalaya

DIRECTIONS

In a 3-inch-high pan, heat butter and oil. Add onions and brown. Add kielbasa and brown. Add sausage and brown. Add chicken breasts, mushrooms and beans. Turn. Once mixture is brown enough, add broth and jambalaya mix. Stir and bring to a boil. Turn heat down to a simmer and cover. Cook about 30 minutes or until liquid reduces.

INGREDIENTS

2 tablespoons butter

3 tablespoons olive oil

2 onions, diced

1 (16-ounce) package kielbasa, cut into quarters

2 whole, boneless chicken breasts, boiled and pulled apart into small pieces

1/2 pound loose hot or sweet sausage, pulled apart into small pieces

2 (4-ounce) cans mushrooms or 1 (8-ounce) box fresh

2 (14 1/2-ounce) cans french cut green beans

2 (14 1/2-ounce) cans beef broth

1 (8-ounce) box jambalaya mix

SUBMITTED BY:
Dave Correia, Robinson

Ham a la King

DIRECTIONS

In a deep skillet, cook onion and green pepper in butter until tender. Blend in remaining ingredients. Heat and stir occasionally. Serve over cooked rice. Makes 2 1/2 cups.

INGREDIENTS

1/4 cup chopped onion

2 tablespoons chopped green pepper

2 tablespoons butter or shortening

1 (10 3/4-ounce) can cream of chicken mushroom soup

1/3 cup milk

1/8 teaspoon dry mustard

1 1/2 cups cubed, cooked ham

2 tablespoons diced pimiento

SUBMITTED BY:
Cheryl Fox, Boardman

Harvest Dinner

DIRECTIONS

Preheat oven to 350 degrees. Fry sausage in a skillet until crumbly and light brown; remove from pan. Fry bacon until crisp; remove from pan and crumble. Drain all but 3 tablespoons pan drippings. Sauté onions till soft; add cabbage and cook 5 minutes. Add apples, cooking until soft. Return sausage and crumbled bacon to pan. Season mixture with white pepper and kosher salt. Place skillet in oven for 10 minutes. Serve with pumpernickel bread and a salad.

INGREDIENTS

1/2 pound loose sweet Italian sausage

1/2 pound bacon

1/2 cup chopped onions

1/2 head cabbage, coarsely chopped

1 gala apple

1/2 teaspoon white pepper

1 teaspoon kosher salt

Pumpernickel bread, for serving

SUBMITTED BY:
Cay Welch, Blairsville

Hearty Italian Soup

DIRECTIONS

In a Dutch oven or large saucepan, brown sausage, green pepper and onion; drain. Stir in remaining ingredients, except macaroni and cheese. Cover; simmer 15 minutes. Stir in pasta; cover and simmer 10 to 12 minutes or until pasta is tender. Serve individual portions topped with choice of cheese.

INGREDIENTS

1 pound bulk mild or hot Italian pork sausage

1 medium green pepper, chopped

1 medium onion, chopped

1 (28-ounce) can diced tomatoes

2 (8-ounce) cans tomato sauce

2 (8-ounce) cans water

1 tablespoon granulated (or 3 cubes) chicken bouillon

3/4 teaspoon garlic salt

3/4 cup small, shaped pasta

Shredded mozzarella, cheddar or American cheese, for garnishing

SUBMITTED BY:
Carol Zanella, Verona

Merica's
HOME COOKING

Kale Sausage Soup

DIRECTIONS

In a large saucepan, sauté onion and garlic in oil until tender. Add broth, potatoes, salt and pepper. Bring to a boil. Reduce heat; cover and simmer for 10 to 15 minutes or until potatoes are tender. Using a potato masher, mash potatoes slightly. Add kale, beans and sausage, cook over medium-low heat until kale is tender. Serves 6 to 7.

INGREDIENTS

3/4 cup chopped onion

2 cloves garlic, minced

1 tablespoon olive oil

4 cups chicken broth

2 medium potatoes, peeled and cubed

1/4 teaspoon salt

1/4 teaspoon pepper

1 pound fresh kale, trimmed and chopped

1 (15-ounce) can cannellini or navy beans

1/2 pound polish or turkey kielbasa, sliced

SUBMITTED BY:
Terry Kratafil, Jacksonville

Kielbasa with Pasta and Baked Beans

DIRECTIONS

In a large skillet, sauté the onion in butter and oil until tender. Add sausage; cook for 2 to 3 minutes, stirring occasionally. Stir in the remaining ingredients. Bring to a boil. Reduce heat; cover and simmer for 10 to 15 minutes or until heated through. Serve with Italian or French bread slices and a tossed salad. Serves 4 to 6.

INGREDIENTS

1/2 cup chopped onion

1 tablespoon butter

2 teaspoons vegetable oil

1 pound cooked kielbasa or polish sausage, cut into 1/8-inch slices

1 (28-ounce) can pork and beans

1 cup cooked elbow macaroni or rotelle pasta

1 cup ketchup

2 tablespoons Worcestershire sauce

1 tablespoon steak sauce

SUBMITTED BY:

Lois Richardson, Springdale

Kielbasa with Rice

DIRECTIONS

In a large skillet, combine soup, water, butter, salt, pepper and Italian seasonings. Bring to a boil. Add kielbasa and rice. Reduce heat, cover and simmer for 18 minutes. Add peas and mushrooms; mix well. Cover and cook for another 15 minutes or until rice is tender. Uncover and sprinkle cheese over the rice mixture. Cover, remove from heat and let cheese melt. Serves 4 to 6.

INGREDIENTS

1 (10 3/4-ounce) can cream of celery soup

1 1/2 cups water

1 tablespoon butter, melted

1/2 teaspoon each salt and pepper

1 teaspoon Italian seasoning

1 pound smoked kielbasa, cut into 1/2-inch pieces

3/4 cup uncooked rice

1 (10-ounce) box frozen peas

1 (4 1/2-ounce) jar sliced mushrooms, drained

1 cup shredded cheddar cheese

SUBMITTED BY:
Kevin Sunderlin, DuBois

One-Pan Sausage and Vegetables

Directions

Preheat oven to 350 degrees. Line bottom of roaster pan with potatoes and carrots. Add sausage and top with peppers. Bake for 1 hour. Remove from oven and let sit for 10 minutes.

Note

This dish makes its own sauce and the peppers add nice color on top.

Ingredients

3 unpeeled sweet potatoes, cut into 1-inch chunks

8 unpeeled small white potatoes, cut into 1-inch chunks

8 unpeeled small red potatoes, cut into 1-inch chunks

4 carrots, peeled and cut into 1-inch chunks

1 pound sweet or hot sausage links, cut into 1-inch chunks

Assorted sweet peppers (red, yellow, green), cut into circles

Submitted by:
Donna Bird, Hanover Township

One-Pot Pork and Rice

DIRECTIONS

Preheat oven to 350 degrees. In a Dutch oven, brown both sides of pork chops in oil; drain. Remove chops from pan and layer rice, onion and green pepper in Dutch oven. Top with pork chops. Combine gravy mix, tomatoes and water. Pour over chops. Cover and bake in oven for 1 hour.

INGREDIENTS

6 (5-ounce) boneless pork loin chops

2 teaspoons canola oil

1 cup uncooked long-grain rice

1 large onion, sliced

1 large green pepper, sliced

1 (3/4-ounce) envelope pork gravy mix

1 (28-ounce) can diced tomatoes, undrained

1 1/2 cups water

SUBMITTED BY:
Betty Pandullo, Blairsville

America's
HOME COOKING

One-Pot Pork Chops

DIRECTIONS

Coat pork chops with flour. In a large skillet, brown both sides of chops. Add potatoes, carrots and green beans. In a small bowl, combine water, Worcestershire sauce, salt and oregano; pour over pork and vegetables. Cover and simmer for 25 minutes. Stir in the soup; cover and simmer 10 to 15 minutes longer or until meat and vegetables are tender. Can be served with toasted bread and coleslaw. Serves 4 to 6.

INGREDIENTS

4 to 6 (6-ounce) boneless pork chops

1/4 cup all-purpose flour

6 small potatoes, quartered

1 cup fresh baby carrots, sliced in half

1 cup frozen green beans, slightly thawed

1/2 cup water

2 teaspoons Worcestershire sauce

1/2 teaspoon salt

1/4 teaspoon oregano

1 (10 3/4-ounce) can condensed tomato soup, undiluted

SUBMITTED BY:
Lois Richardson, Springdale

Pepperoni Pizza Pork Chops

DIRECTIONS

Preheat oven to 400 degrees. Season pork chops with salt, pepper and oregano. In a large, deep ovenproof skillet, sauté pork chops in olive oil for 3 to 5 minutes on each side. Remove from skillet and set aside. Sauté 1/2 cup diced pepperoni, red onion and red pepper, reserving 2 tablespoons red pepper for garnishing. Add spaghetti sauce and black olives. Add tortellini and heat through. Place pork chops on top of tortellini and spoon sauce over top of pork chops. Sprinkle with mozzarella cheese. Top with remaining pepperoni and bell pepper. Put entire skillet into oven and heat until cheese melts, approximately 5 to 10 minutes. Remove from oven and top with parmesan cheese.

INGREDIENTS

4 boneless pork chops, pounded thin

Salt, pepper and oregano, to taste

2 tablespoons olive oil

1 stick pepperoni, sliced and diced

1/2 red onion

1 red bell pepper

2 cups spaghetti sauce

1 (6-ounce) can sliced black olives

1 (8-ounce) bag shredded mozzarella cheese

1 (8-ounce) package fresh cheese-filled tortellini

Parmesan cheese, to taste

SUBMITTED BY:
Monica Narr, Crafton

Pittsburgh Pot of Yoy

DIRECTIONS

In an 8-quart pot, combine kielbasa, sauerkraut, beans with juice, potato soup, potatoes, caraway seeds and beer or broth. Heat on medium until hot and just bubbly. Meanwhile, cook noodles according to package directions; drain. To serve, put noodles in individual bowls and then ladle on the "Yoy." Serve with buttered rye bread or pumpernickel. Serves 6.

INGREDIENTS

1 pound kielbasa, sliced 1/4 inch thick and then cut in half

1 (15-ounce) can sauerkraut, drained and rinsed

1 (15-ounce) can cannellini beans

1 (15-ounce) can potato soup

1 cup leftover cubed or mashed potatoes

1 tablespoon caraway seeds

2 cups beer or chicken broth

1 (8-ounce) package wide noodles, cooked and drained

SUBMITTED BY:
Chris Bobick, Chalk Hill

Pork and Pineapple Stir-Fry

DIRECTIONS

Combine first 7 ingredients and set aside. Heat 1 teaspoon oil over medium-high heat in a large nonstick skillet coated with cooking spray. Add pork and stir-fry for 4 minutes. Remove pork from pan and set aside. Heat 1 teaspoon oil in pan, add onions and bell pepper, and stir-fry 5 minutes or until vegetables are tender. Add ginger and garlic and cook 30 seconds. Return pork to pan; add broth mixture and pineapple, and stir-fry 3 minutes or until thoroughly heated. Serve over rice. Serves 4.

INGREDIENTS

1 cup beef broth

1/4 cup tomato paste

1 tablespoon low-sodium soy sauce

2 teaspoons cornstarch

2 teaspoons brown sugar

2 teaspoons curry powder

1/4 teaspoon chili powder

2 teaspoons vegetable oil, divided

Nonstick cooking spray

1 pound pork tenderloin, cut into short, thin strips

1 cup sliced onion

1 cup green bell pepper

2 teaspoons peeled and minced fresh ginger

1 1/2 teaspoons minced garlic

1 (15 1/4-ounce) can light pineapple chunks, drained

4 cups cooked instant rice

SUBMITTED BY:
Sharon Lemasters, Morgantown

64

Pork Chop Casserole

DIRECTIONS

Fry pork chops in oil. Remove from pan. Add onion and fry until golden brown. Scrape bottom of pan to loosen bits of meat and onion. Add 1 can each of soup and water. Add potatoes to pan. Add pork chops back to skillet and season to taste. Cover and cook for 1/2 hour. Remove lid and continue cooking until potatoes are tender.

NOTE

Add more water to soup if water seems to be evaporating. This dish can also be baked in the oven with lid on, for about 1 hour.

INGREDIENTS

4 to 5 pork chops

1 medium onion, chopped

1 (10 1/2-ounce) can cream of garlic or regular mushroom soup

1 (10 1/2-ounce) can water

4 to 5 potatoes, peeled and sliced

SUBMITTED BY:

Jan LaFever, Pittsburgh

America's HOME COOKING

Pork Chop Skillet Dinner

DIRECTIONS

Brown chops in shortening; pour off excess fat. On each chop, place a tablespoon of rice, a slice of onion and green pepper, and 1/2 cup of tomatoes. Season and cover with liquid from tomatoes. Cover and cook over low heat until chops are tender, about 1 hour.

INGREDIENTS

4 pork chops

1 tablespoon shortening

4 tablespoons uncooked instant rice

4 slices onion

4 slices green pepper

2 cups canned tomatoes

1 teaspoon salt

1/2 teaspoon pepper

2 tablespoons oil

SUBMITTED BY:
Dwight and Ruth Troup, Plum

66

Pork Chop Supper

DIRECTIONS

In a large skillet, brown chops in oil; drain and remove. In skillet, combine water, rice, onions and 1/2 teaspoon salt. Return pork chops to skillet; top with corn and tomatoes. Sprinkle with remaining salt and pepper; bring to a boil. Reduce to a simmer and cover. Cook 20 to 25 minutes or until chops and rice are tender. Let stand 5 minutes.

Serve with salad, crusty bread and apple pie. Serves 4.

INGREDIENTS

4 1/2-inch-thick pork chops

2 tablespoons vegetable oil

1 1/4 cups water

2/3 cups uncooked rice

1/2 cup chopped onions

1 teaspoon salt, divided

1 (15-ounce) can whole kernel corn, drained

1 (14 1/2-ounce) can diced tomatoes

1/4 teaspoon black pepper

SUBMITTED BY:
Kevin Sunderlin, DuBois

Pork Chops with Peppers and Rice

DIRECTIONS

Parboil rice for five minutes; set aside. Brown chops in a skillet with tight-fitting lid. Place 1 onion slice on top of each pork chop, add 1 pepper ring on each onion slice and finally place 1/4 cup of rice in the center of each pepper ring. Pour tomatoes and juice around pork chops. Spoon a small amount on rice to moisten. Bring skillet to a simmer. Cover and continue to simmer on low for 45 minutes or until rice is steamed. Carefully lift each chop to plate. Serve with tomato sauce from the skillet.

INGREDIENTS

1 cup white rice

4 center-cut pork chops

4 1/4-inch slices large sweet onions

4 1-inch-round slices green pepper

4 cups canned chopped tomatoes with juice

Salt and pepper, to taste

SUBMITTED BY:
Pat Prohaska, Bradenville

Pork, Potatoes and Sauerkraut in Pressure

Directions

In bottom of pressure cooker, sauté bacon for 3 to 5 minutes. Add oil and onions and sauté for about 8 to 10 minutes until onions are translucent. With a slotted spoon, remove onions and bacon; add pork and lightly brown, about 5 to 8 minutes. Add bacon, onions and sauerkraut with its juice to the pork. Make sure you have about 1 inch of liquid—if not, add a little water. Pressure cook for 35 minutes. Depressurize; add potatoes, salt, pepper and sugar. Mix well and pressure cook for 10 minutes. Serves 4.

Ingredients

3 strips bacon, chopped

4 tablespoons canola, peanut, olive or other oil

2 medium onions, chopped

3 1/2 pounds boneless spareribs, chops or pork roast, cut into cubes

2 pounds sauerkraut

6 medium potatoes, cubed

1 teaspoon salt

1/2 teaspoon pepper

1 tablespoon sugar

SUBMITTED BY:
Richard Rajter, Ambridge

America's
HOME COOKING

Pork Scaloppini with Angel Hair Zinfandel

DIRECTIONS

Heat oil in a deep skillet. Salt and pepper pork and then bread medallions by dredging in flour, then egg and finally in breadcrumbs. Fry in oil until crispy and brown. Drain on paper towel and set aside. Place the vegetables in pan and begin to lightly sauté until they are wilted and lightly cooked. Add broth and reduce cooking liquid slightly. Add wine and adjust seasonings (salt, pepper and sugar), according to taste. The sauce should be slightly tart and slightly sweet from the wine. Add pasta to cooking liquid and cook until al dente, about 5 minutes. Add crispy pork medallions and toss. Serve with parmigiano reggiano cheese curls and fresh basil on top.

INGREDIENTS

1/2 cup vegetable oil or a combination of olive and vegetable oils

Salt and pepper, to taste

1 (1-pound) pork tenderloin, cut into thin medallions

1/2 cup flour, for dredging

1 egg, beaten

1/2 cup Italian breadcrumbs and 1/2 cup parmesan cheese, mixed together

1 medium green pepper, cut into long slices

1 medium red pepper, cut into long slices

1 (8-ounce) package sliced mushrooms

1 medium sweet onion, sliced

1 clove garlic, minced

2 (14-ounce) cans beef broth

1 cup white zinfandel wine

1/2 teaspoon sugar

1 pound angel hair pasta

Parmigiano reggiano cheese, sliced into curls, for garnishing

Fresh basil, for garnishing

SUBMITTED BY:
Nina Mule Lyons, Pittsburgh

Pulled Pork BBQ

DIRECTIONS

Place meat in a slow cooker. Add water and bouillon. Season with garlic powder and salt and pepper. Cook on high for 4 to 6 hours or until meat is very tender. Remove meat from slow cooker and set aside to cool slightly. Discard liquid. Shred meat with fingers, discarding any fat and bones. Return meat to slow cooker. Add remaining ingredients and stir well. Cook on high for 30 minutes to 1 hour more. (If left unattended for more than 1 hour, set slow cooker to low.) Stir well again and serve on whole wheat buns.

INGREDIENTS

1 (3- to 5-pound) pork roast or mixed pork pieces (center-cut and sirloin chops)

4 cups water

3 chicken or beef bouillon cubes

Garlic powder, to taste

Coarse or kosher salt, to taste

Fresh ground black pepper, to taste

1 (12-ounce) bottle chili sauce

2 to 3 tablespoons honey

1 tablespoon yellow mustard

1 teaspoon dry mustard

4 to 6 dashes soy sauce

2/3 cup dark brown sugar

1 cup ketchup

1 tablespoon apple cider vinegar

5 dashes hot sauce

1 (12-ounce) package whole wheat kaiser rolls

SUBMITTED BY:
Patty Seaman, Coraopolis

America's
HOME COOKING

Sandra's Sizzling Fiesta Salad

DIRECTIONS

Heat oil in a skillet and sauté onion rings. Cut sausage into 1/2- to 1-inch diagonal slices and add to onions, cooking until done. While sausage cooks, rinse and dry fresh salad blend. Stir in Italian dressing and arrange on platter. Turn off heat under sausage; pour off fat. Add corn and warm for 1 minute. With a slotted spoon, place sausage and corn on the salad greens, then top with drained salsa. Serve with tortilla chips, Italian bread, bread sticks, or biscuits or rolls.

INGREDIENTS

2 tablespoons vegetable oil

1 small to medium onion, sliced into thin rings

16 ounces sausage

8 to 12 ounces fresh salad blend

1/4 cup Italian salad dressing

2 (11- or 16-ounce) cans of corn, drained

1 (12-ounce) jar salsa, drained

SUBMITTED BY:
Sandra Gould Ford, Pittsburgh

Sausage, Pepper and Potato Skillet

DIRECTIONS

Brown sausage on all sides in a deep 12-inch skillet, about 10 minutes. Drain all but 2 tablespoons drippings. Stir in onion, peppers, potatoes, water and black pepper. Reduce heat to low, cover and cook 15 to 20 minutes or until potatoes are tender. Serves 4.

INGREDIENTS

1 pound Italian link sausage, sliced 1-inch thick

1 medium onion, cut in 1-inch cubes

1 large green pepper, cut in 1-inch cubes

1 large sweet red pepper, diced

1 1/4 pounds small new potatoes, cut in 3/4-inch cubes

3/4 cup water

1/8 teaspoon pepper

SUBMITTED BY:
Sandra Adams, Pittsburgh

America's
HOME COOKING

Skillet Breakfast Casserole

DIRECTIONS

In a large nonstick skillet, cook bacon or sausage until done. Remove to paper towels and drain. Remove excess drippings from pan and add butter or margarine. Scrub potatoes, leaving skins on. Using a food processor, mandolin or sharp knife, slice the potatoes about 1/4 inch thick. Add potatoes to skillet by starting in the center and working out in a circle, overlapping to cover the bottom of the skillet and part way up the sides. Toss the chopped onions on the potatoes and season with salt and pepper. Cover skillet and reduce heat to medium-low. When potatoes are cooked through, add beaten eggs, bacon or sausage, and top with cheese. Cook 10 to 15 minutes on medium-low until eggs are cooked and cheese is melted.

INGREDIENTS

4 slices bacon or sausage links, diced

4 medium red-skinned potatoes

1 teaspoon butter or margarine

1/2 small onion, diced

1/4 teaspoon salt

1/4 teaspoon pepper

3 eggs, lightly beaten

1 cup shredded cheese of choice

SUBMITTED BY:
Kimberlee Love, North Side

74

Skillet Kielbasa and Pierogies

Directions

Melt butter in a large skillet and add cabbage and onion. Cook until soft, stirring frequently. Add kielbasa and cook covered for 10 minutes. Add pierogies and stir gently to mix. Season to taste and serve.

Ingredients

1/2 cup (1 stick) butter

1 head cabbage, chopped

1 onion, chopped

1 pound kielbasa, sliced into 1/2-inch pieces

1 (14-ounce) box potato and cheddar pierogies, boiled according to package directions

Salt and pepper, to taste

Submitted by:
Sharon Cercone, McKees Rocks

Skillet Sausage and Beans

DIRECTIONS

Place a large skillet over medium heat. Brown sausage. If using rope sausage, cut into serving pieces after browning. Add garbanzo beans and enough liquid to almost cover sausage. Add onion. Bring to a boil, reduce heat, cover and simmer 30 to 45 minutes, stirring occasionally, until sausage is cooked through and garbanzo beans are tender. Season with salt and pepper and serve.

INGREDIENTS

1 pound hot or sweet Italian sausage in casing

2 (15-ounce) cans garbanzo beans with liquid

1 large yellow onion, cut into large chunks

Salt and pepper, to taste

SUBMITTED BY:
Erin DeCaro, Hempfield Township

Smoked Chops and Potatoes

DIRECTIONS

In a large skillet, cook potatoes, onion and frozen vegetables in a small amount of boiling water for 8 minutes or until tender. Drain vegetables in colander. In the same skillet, place margarine or oil on low heat and lightly brown pork chops on each side. Place potatoes and vegetables over chops and spoon gravy over all. Cover and cook over low-medium heat for 7 to 8 minutes or until heated through. Makes 4 servings.

INGREDIENTS

3 medium potatoes, sliced

1 small onion, diced

1 cup frozen broccoli, cauliflower and carrots

4 smoked pork chops, cut 1/2 to 1/4 inch thick

1 (12-ounce) jar brown gravy

1 teaspoon margarine or oil

SUBMITTED BY:

JoAnn Hilliard, East Liverpool

America's
HOME COOKING

Sweet and Sour Meatballs

DIRECTIONS

In a large skillet, brown sausage balls and drain fat. Meanwhile, combine pineapple liquid, lemon juice, soy sauce, ginger and brown sugar. In a small cup, mix 2 tablespoons lemon mixture with cornstarch; set aside. Add remaining lemon mixture to skillet, cover and simmer 20 to 25 minutes. Add pineapple and green pepper and heat through. Gradually stir in cornstarch mixture; bring to a boil and stir for 1 minute. Place in serving dish. Serve with rice or noodles, if desired.

INGREDIENTS

2 pounds bulk sausage, rolled into 1 1/2-inch balls

2 (20-ounce) cans chunked pineapple, drained, reserving 1 cup liquid

1 cup real lemon juice

2 tablespoons soy sauce

1 teaspoon ground ginger

1/3 cup firmly packed light brown sugar

2 tablespoons cornstarch

2 medium green peppers, chopped

SUBMITTED BY:
Mary Vraninin, Langeloth

Tarragon Mustard Pork Chops

DIRECTIONS

In a small bowl, whisk together vinegar, mustard, tarragon, garlic and sugar; season with pepper. Brown pork chops in a skillet. Spread 1 tablespoon of vinegar mixture on each chop. Sprinkle with onion. Add carrots and potatoes. Pour remaining vinegar mixture on top. Add water. Cover and cook for 30 to 40 minutes or until the potatoes and carrots are cooked to taste. This dish also can be baked in the oven.

INGREDIENTS

1/4 cup red wine vinegar

2 tablespoons mustard

1 teaspoon dried tarragon

1 to 2 garlic cloves, minced

2 teaspoons sugar or 1 package sugar substitute

Pepper, to taste

2 pork chops

1/2 small onion, chopped

2 potatoes, cut into 1/4- or 1/2-inch slices

2 carrots, cut into 1/2-inch slices

2 tablespoons water

SUBMITTED BY:

Diane Pavlick, New Kensington

Wieners and Potatoes

DIRECTIONS

Slice hot dogs, kielbasa or sausage into "rings" and place in electric skillet. Add onions and sauté in oil until onions are translucent. Top with sliced potatoes. Cover all with water. Season with seasoning blend and add enough Hungarian paprika to turn water red in color. Set electric skillet to 350 degrees and cook until potatoes are tender and broth cooks down to a light gravy. Serve in bowls. Serves 4 to 6.

INGREDIENTS

1 pound hot dogs, kielbasa, or sweet or hot sausage

1/4 cup mixed vegetable and olive oils

1 large sweet onion, chopped

6 medium Idaho potatoes, thinly sliced

Natural seasoning blend

Hungarian paprika

SUBMITTED BY:
Nancy Simon, Beaver Falls

ONE SKILLET

Poultry

Chicken and Tri-Color Peppers

DIRECTIONS

Cover chicken with olive oil and season with minced garlic. Sauté chicken in skillet. Add peppers and cover for a few minutes to steam and soften. Be careful not to discolor the peppers. Serve chicken over rice. This dish reheats well and leftovers can be used as a cold salad.

VARIATION

Omit rice and serve with cooked potatoes, or add Oriental ingredients, such as snow peas, water chestnuts or mushrooms, if desired.

INGREDIENTS

Olive oil

Minced garlic, to taste

4 skinless, boneless chicken breasts, diced

1 each red, yellow and green bell pepper, julienned

Snow peas (optional)

Water chestnuts (optional)

Mushrooms (optional)

SUBMITTED BY:
Carleen Kemble, Pittsburgh

Chicken Bog

DIRECTIONS

In a stockpot, combine chicken, sausage, onion, butter, seasonings and bay leaves. Add water and bring to a boil. Cover and cook at a low boil for 40 minutes. Remove chicken and cool slightly. Add rice to liquid in stockpot. Bring to a boil, stirring well. Boil for 10 minutes and then reduce heat, cover and simmer 10 minutes or until rice is done. (Note: Do not put lid on tight. Leave a small space for steam to escape.) While rice is cooking, pick chicken apart, discarding skin and bones. When rice is cooked, remove bay leaves and return chicken to the pot; stir well.

INGREDIENTS

1 (3-pound) chicken, quartered

1 pound smoked link sausage, sliced into 1/2-inch pieces

1 cup chopped onions

1/2 cup (1 stick) butter

2 teaspoons seasoning salt

1 teaspoon salt

1 teaspoon black pepper

1 teaspoon garlic powder

1 teaspoon ground red pepper

3 bay leaves

8 cups water

3 cups raw white rice

SUBMITTED BY:
Terry Kratafil, Jacksonville

America's
HOME COOKING

Chicken Fricasse

DIRECTIONS

Wash cut chicken in water and then soak in salt water until needed. In a 12-inch Dutch oven, sauté onions, garlic and celery in olive oil until soft. Add the drained chicken pieces and simmer 10 minutes on each side. Add crushed tomatoes, stirring well. Add the seasonings, sage leaves and vinegar. Stir in potatoes and cover; simmer for 1 hour or until potatoes and chicken are fork tender. Gently stir in peas and cover. Cook for 5 more minutes. Serve with homemade bread.

INGREDIENTS

1 whole fryer chicken, cut into serving-size pieces

2 tablespoons olive oil

1 large onion, diced

6 cloves garlic, minced

3 large stalks celery, diced

1 (28-ounce) can crushed tomatoes

Salt and pepper, to taste

1/8 teaspoon fresh ground nutmeg and 1 teaspoon fresh ground cinnamon or 1 teaspoon finely chopped fresh rosemary

8 sage leaves, finely chopped

2 tablespoons apple cider vinegar

4 potatoes, quartered

1 (15-ounce) can sweet peas

SUBMITTED BY:
Denise Wolf, Elizabeth

Chicken Italiano

DIRECTIONS

Preheat oven to 350 degrees. In a small bowl, thoroughly combine flour, butter, salad dressing mix and paprika. Blend in water. Spread butter mixture over chicken. Spray a 9x13-inch baking dish with cooking spray. Place chicken in baking dish then coat with butter mixture. Add 1/4 cup water. Cover and bake for 45 minutes. Remove cover and bake 15 minutes more.

INGREDIENTS

1/4 cup all-purpose flour

2 tablespoons softened butter

1 (3/4-ounce) envelope Italian dressing mix

1/2 teaspoon paprika

3 tablespoons water

Nonstick cooking spray

4 boneless chicken breasts or 1 (2-pound) whole chicken, cut into pieces

1/4 cup water

SUBMITTED BY:
Lori Ann Predmore, Lincoln University

Chicken or Turkey and Rice Casserole

DIRECTIONS

Combine all ingredients, except cheese, in a 1 1/2-quart microwave-proof dish. Cover with plastic wrap. Use cook cycle and cook 20 to 25 minutes in microwave. Stir twice during cooking time. Sprinkle with cheese. Cover and let stand 10 minutes before serving.

INGREDIENTS

2 cups cooked, cubed chicken or turkey

1 (10 3/4-ounce) can condensed cream of chicken soup

1 cup milk

1 cup quick-cooking rice

1/2 teaspoon poultry seasoning

1 cup sliced mushrooms

1 cup frozen peas

1/2 cup shredded cheese of choice

SUBMITTED BY:
Cindy Hilliard, East Liverpool

Chicken Risotto

DIRECTIONS

In a large skillet, melt 2 tablespoons of butter. Add chicken strips and cook until pieces are browned, about 5 to 8 minutes, stirring constantly. Remove chicken and add remaining butter, uncooked rice and minced garlic to skillet and cook, stirring constantly until rice is lightly browned, about 5 minutes. Add mushrooms and green onions and continue cooking, stirring occasionally, until mushrooms are tender, about 3 to 4 minutes. Stir in chicken broth and Italian seasoning. Bring to a boil; cover and simmer 15 minutes. Gently stir chicken back into skillet and continue simmering until chicken is heated through and rice is tender, about 5 minutes. Top with cheese and serve. Makes 4 to 5 servings.

INGREDIENTS

6 tablespoons butter

1 pound boneless chicken breasts, cut into thin strips

1 1/2 cups uncooked long-grain rice

2 cloves garlic, minced

1/2 pound mushrooms, sliced

4 green onions, sliced

3 cups chicken broth

1 teaspoon Italian seasoning

1 1/2 cups shredded cheddar cheese

SUBMITTED BY:
Donna Sunday, Pittsburgh

America's
HOME COOKING

Chicken Risotto and Vegetables

DIRECTIONS

Heat butter and oil in a deep 12-inch skillet. Add chicken; sauté about 5 minutes. Season chicken with salt and pepper; transfer to a plate and set aside. Add onion to skillet and sauté 5 minutes. Stir in rice and broth. Cover and bring to a boil. Reduce heat to low and simmer 10 minutes. Stir in cauliflower, carrots and celery. Cover and simmer 5 minutes. Return chicken to pan, add tomatoes and green beans or asparagus. Cover and simmer 5 minutes more. Remove from heat. Stir in cheese and basil and serve.

INGREDIENTS

2 tablespoons butter

2 tablespoons olive oil

1 pound skinless, boneless chicken breasts, cut into 1-inch cubes

Salt and pepper, to taste

1 medium onion, chopped

1 1/2 cups white rice

2 cups canned chicken broth mixed with 1 cup water

1/2 (10-ounce) package frozen cauliflower, thawed

2 medium carrots, diced

1 celery stalk, diced

1 cup canned diced tomatoes, drained

1/2 (5-ounce) package frozen green beans or asparagus, thawed, drained and chopped

1/2 cup parmesan cheese

2 tablespoons minced fresh basil or parsley

SUBMITTED BY:
Sandra Adams, Pittsburgh

Chicken Stew

DIRECTIONS

Marinate chicken in teriyaki sauce and ginger overnight. Bake in a 350-degree oven for 35 to 40 minutes. Cool and cut into cubes. In a large pot, cook onion and garlic in a little olive oil until translucent. Add remaining ingredients, stir and simmer on low heat for 35 to 45 minutes. Stir about every 5 minutes to prevent sticking or burning. (35 minutes yields very crisp vegetables.) This dish can be eaten as a stew or used as filling for pot pies.

INGREDIENTS

1 skinless chicken breast

1 (12- or 16-ounce) bottle teriyaki sauce, for marinading

1 tablespoon crystallized ginger bits

1/2 small onion, minced

3 to 4 cloves garlic, minced

1 (10 3/4-ounce) can 98% fat-free cream of mushroom soup

1 (10 3/4-ounce) can 98% fat-free cream of chicken soup

1 (16-ounce) bag frozen soup vegetables

1 (4-ounce) can mushroom pieces

1/2 teaspoon tarragon

1/2 teaspoon sweet marjoram

Frozen or fresh broccoli or cauliflower (optional), if not included in bag of soup vegetables

SUBMITTED BY:

Deborah Harding, Swissvale

91

Chicken, Turkey or Shrimp Jambalaya

DIRECTIONS

Sauté garlic, pepper and onion in butter or margarine. Add sausage and shrimp, chicken or ham. Add tomatoes, water and seasonings; bring to a boil. Stir in uncooked rice and reduce heat to simmer. Cover and cook until rice is fluffy. Serves 6.

INGREDIENTS

3 tablespoons butter or margarine

2 cloves garlic, sliced

1 medium green pepper, cut in pieces

1 small onion, quartered

4 to 6 pre-cooked pork sausages

2 to 3 cups whole shrimp, cut-up chicken or diced ham

1 (28-ounce) can whole tomatoes, diced

2 cups water

1 bay leaf

1 teaspoon salt

1/8 teaspoon pepper

Dash red pepper

1 cup uncooked rice

SUBMITTED BY:
Evelyn Hylva, Greensburg

America's HOME COOKING

Commish's Chicken Cacciatore Dish

DIRECTIONS

Heat oil in a large, deep skillet. Sauté chicken, garlic and wine vinegar until chicken is firm and white. Remove and reserve chicken; cover. Add celery, onion, anchovy, basil, oregano, and salt and pepper. Simmer, covered, until celery is soft, adding red wine as needed. Add chicken broth and tomatoes to pan and continue to simmer. Add chicken, remaining wine and cayenne pepper, if desired; place on low heat, stirring occasionally for 30 minutes.

INGREDIENTS

1/2 cup olive oil

3 pounds boneless chicken breasts, cut into strips and chunks

2 cloves garlic, minced

2 tablespoons wine vinegar

1 cup chopped celery

1 cup chopped onion

3 fillets anchovy (optional)

2 tablespoons basil

2 tablespoons oregano

Salt and pepper, to taste

1 cup red wine

1 (14 1/2-ounce) can chicken broth

2 (14 1/2-ounce) cans diced tomatoes

Dash cayenne pepper (optional)

SUBMITTED BY:

Jim Scahill, Armstrong County

America's
HOME COOKING

93

Commish's Curry Lime Chicken Dish

DIRECTIONS

Combine white (or black) pepper and flour in bag and mix by shaking. Add chicken and coat evenly. Reserve excess flour. In deep, large skillet, warm oil to medium-high heat. Add chicken and cook until golden brown all over. Remove chicken to plate and cover. Add onion and garlic to skillet and cook 2 minutes. Add reserved flour and continue stirring until smooth. Add chicken broth, curry powder and hot sauce, bringing mixture to a boil. Reduce heat to low, cover and simmer. In a small bowl, finely grate zest from fresh lime and then add lime juice and cilantro. Increase heat to medium high and bring mixture to a boil. Stir in lime mixture and sour cream. Return chicken and any juices to skillet. Return to boil and cook until chicken is coated and done, about 5 to 7 minutes.

INGREDIENTS

White pepper, if available

2 tablespoons flour

2 pounds chicken thighs

2 tablespoons olive oil

1 large red or Spanish onion, chopped

2 cloves garlic, minced

1 cup chicken broth

3 teaspoons curry powder

Dash hot sauce

1 lime, for zest

1/4 cup lime juice

Fresh cilantro springs, if available

1/2 cup sour cream

SUBMITTED BY:
Jim Scahill, Armstrong County

Commish's Skillet Cock-a-Leekie

DIRECTIONS

Cut chickens into strips and then some strips into pieces. When cutting leeks, use only white and lowest green part of leek. Clean and cut leek into 1/2-inch medallions; reserve. In a large, deep skillet, heat oil to medium-high and add chicken; cook until chicken is white. Make space in the center of skillet and add celery, onions and leeks with small amount of water. Add garlic, salt and pepper. Dust dish all over with flour. Add half of wine and reduce heat. Add carrots. Simmer 5 minutes. Add broth and rest of wine. Bring to a boil and add rice. Return to a boil; reduce heat and cover. Stir occasionally until rice is tender. Serves 5 to 6.

INGREDIENTS

2 pounds boneless chicken breasts

1 large leek, cleaned and cut into 1/2-inch slices

3 tablespoons olive oil

6 stalks celery, chopped in 1/4-inch pieces

1 large sweet onion, chopped

2 cloves garlic, minced

Salt and butcher pepper, to taste

1/2 cup flour, sifted

1 cup white wine

2 to 3 carrots, shredded

2 cups chicken broth

1 cup rice

SUBMITTED BY:
Jim Scahill, Armstrong County

Easy Chicken and Dumplings

DIRECTIONS

Remove skin and fat from chicken. Pull meat from bones and cut into large pieces; set aside for later. In a large soup pot or Dutch oven, add butter and place over medium-high heat. When butter is melted, add chopped onions and celery; sauté until soft. Add broth, poultry seasoning, bay leaf, salt and pepper. Bring to a boil. Add frozen vegetables and diced potatoes and return to a boil. Reduce heat to a simmer for 20 minutes and add chicken pieces; continue to simmer while making dumplings. Remove biscuits from the can and place on a piece of waxed paper. Flatten each biscuit slightly, then cut into wedge-shaped quarters. Stir in the chicken gravy to stew. When stew is simmering steadily, drop dumplings into the pot, one at a time. When all dumplings are in the pot, cover with lid and simmer for about 10 minutes.

INGREDIENTS

1 whole pre-roasted chicken

2 tablespoons butter

1 large yellow onion, coarsely chopped

3 to 4 stalks celery, coarsely chopped

1 (48-ounce) can chicken broth

1 teaspoon poultry seasoning

1 bay leaf

1 teaspoon salt

1/2 teaspoon black pepper

1 (16-ounce) bag frozen mixed vegetables

2 potatoes, peeled and cubed

1 (7 1/2-ounce) can refrigerated buttermilk biscuits

1 (10-ounce) jar chicken gravy

SUBMITTED BY:
Carolyn Moschak, West View

Easy Chicken Sauté

DIRECTIONS

While cooking pasta, sauté onions and garlic in olive oil until soft. Add the chicken pieces and stir-fry until opaque. Add artichokes, olives, red pepper pieces and salt. Keep warm until the pasta is cooked; toss drained pasta with the chicken and vegetables in a large warmed serving bowl and sprinkle with grated cheese. Serves 6.

INGREDIENTS

1 pound bow tie pasta

Olive oil

1 large sweet onion, cut into quarters and thickly sliced

2 large cloves garlic, sliced

1 pound boneless chicken breast, cut into 1-inch pieces

2 (6-ounce) jars artichokes with marinade

1 cup black olives, pitted and sliced in half

1 (7 1/2-ounce) jar roasted red peppers, drained and cut into 1-inch pieces

Salt, to taste

1/4 to 1/2 cup freshly grated parmigiano reggiano cheese

SUBMITTED BY:
Carol Shenk, Kittanning

Eleanor's Curried Chicken with Brandy

Directions

In a large, heavy skillet, brown chicken in butter. Add onion. Cover and cook onion and chicken over low heat for 30 minutes or until done. Add a little water if necessary to prevent chicken from burning. Remove chicken to a platter and keep warm. Whisk flour and curry powder into the butter and onion mixture. Cook for 1 to 2 minutes. Stir in heavy cream and apricot brandy and cook, stirring continuously, until mixture thickens. Return chicken to sauce and simmer on low for 10 minutes. Serve with steamed rice and, if desired, garnish with cashews, chutney, toasted coconut and chopped dried apricots.

Note

This recipe can be made less "rich" by substituting either evaporated skim milk or a thick mixture of skim milk powder and water in place of the cream.

Ingredients

8 skinless pieces chicken

1/2 cup butter

1 large onion, chopped

2 tablespoons flour

1 tablespoon curry powder

2 cups heavy cream

1/3 cup apricot brandy

Cashews, chutney, toasted coconut and dried apricots, for garnishing (optional)

SUBMITTED BY:
Carol Blank, Upper St. Clair

Garlic Cheese Chicken

DIRECTIONS

Preheat oven to 350 degrees. Melt butter and add roasted garlic. In a bowl, mix breadcrumbs and all three cheeses together. Dip chicken breasts in butter and garlic and then place breasts in breadcrumbs and cheese. Heap about 1 inch of breadcrumbs and cheese on top of each breasts. Pick up breasts underneath with about 1 inch of breadcrumbs and cheese and place in a greased glass pan. Cook for 45 minutes to 1 hour until brown. Serve with rice.

INGREDIENTS

1/2 cup (1 stick) butter

1 spoonful jarred roasted garlic

Italian breadcrumbs

2 cups mozzarella cheese

2 cups cheddar cheese

1 cup parmesan cheese

3 chicken breasts, cleaned and cut in half

SUBMITTED BY:

Dave Correia, Robinson

99

One-Pot Chicken and Dumplings

DIRECTIONS

Cut chicken into strips and dice into bite-size pieces. In a deep cast-iron skillet, sauté onions until translucent; add green pepper and chicken. Once chicken turns opaque, add tomatoes, Italian seasonings, and salt and pepper. Add chicken stock as needed.

To make dumplings, mix flour, pinch of salt and baking powder in a large bowl. With a whisk, add milk until a semi-thick mixture forms. With a tablespoon, drop the dumpling mixture on top of the chicken. Cover and cook until finished, about 15 minutes.

INGREDIENTS

2 boneless, skinless chicken breasts

1 medium sweet onion, diced

1 green pepper, diced

1 (14 1/2-ounce) can diced tomatoes

Italian seasonings

Salt and pepper, to taste

2 cups flour

1/2 teaspoon baking powder

1 cup milk

6 cups chicken stock

SUBMITTED BY:
John Ladik, Munhall

One-Skillet Ginger Chicken

DIRECTIONS

In a large skillet over medium heat, mix oil and cubed chicken breast. Add about 1/2 teaspoon grated ginger. Brown chicken; set aside. Add 1/8 cup chicken broth to pan. Add green pepper, yellow onion and garlic. Sauté until onions are tender and green pepper is soft. Add oriental vegetables and another 1/4 cup chicken broth; mix well and cover. Let simmer on medium-low heat for about 10 minutes. Add chicken back to skillet and add more ginger to taste. Add sugar, soy sauce, celery and green onions; stir. Add baby corn; stir. When all vegetables are soft and tender, add cornstarch 1 teaspoon at a time, stirring until the sauce thickens. Serve alone or over rice or oriental noodles.

INGREDIENTS

2 tablespoons vegetable oil

1 pound cubed chicken breast

Fresh grated ginger or ginger powder

1 (14 1/5-ounce) can chicken broth

1 medium green pepper, julienned

1 small yellow onion, sliced and cut into half moons

1 to 2 cloves garlic, minced

1 (28-ounce) can oriental vegetables or 1 (8-ounce) can each bean sprouts, water chestnuts and bamboo shoots

1 (15-ounce) can baby corn

1 tablespoon sugar

1/8 cup soy sauce

2 small stalks celery, chopped

3 large green onions, chopped

Cornstarch

SUBMITTED BY:
Clifton Britt, Butler

America's
HOME COOKING

Orange Italian Chicken

DIRECTIONS

In a large skillet or Dutch oven, heat oil. Season diced chicken with salt, pepper and tomato basil garlic. Add chicken to pan and brown; add dried oregano. After chicken is browned, add broccoli florets, orange marmalade and Italian dressing; stir to coat. Cover and simmer for 10 to 15 minutes. Serve over chow mein noodles or on a bed of lettuce or salad greens.

INGREDIENTS

4 tablespoons oil

4 boneless, skinless chicken breasts, diced

Salt and pepper, to taste

2 capfuls tomato basil garlic seasoning

1 teaspoon dried oregano

1 head broccoli, cut into florets

1 (13-ounce) jar orange marmalade

1 (8-ounce) bottle Italian salad dressing

1 (5-ounce) can chow mein noodles, if desired

1 head lettuce or bunch salad greens, if desired

SUBMITTED BY:
Heidi and Monica Narr, Crafton

Quick Chicken Bog

DIRECTIONS

In a large, deep skillet or pot, add chicken broth, onion, butter, seasonings, bay leaves and rice. Bring to a boil, stirring well. Boil for 10 minutes and then add smoked sausage. Reduce heat and cover loosely. Simmer for 10 minutes or until rice is done. When rice is done, add chicken and stir. Remove bay leaves. Serve hot with a tomato, basil and mozzarella salad and fresh bread.

NOTE

If chicken bog seems too dry, add more chicken broth until bog is moist, but not soup.

INGREDIENTS

4 cups chicken broth

1/2 cup chopped onions

1/2 cup (1 stick) butter

1 teaspoon seasoning salt

1/2 teaspoon salt

1/2 teaspoon black pepper

1/2 teaspoon garlic powder

1 teaspoon ground red pepper

2 bay leaves

2 to 3 dashes hot sauce

1/2 pound smoked link sausage

1 1/2 cups raw white rice

2 cups cooked chicken

SUBMITTED BY:
Terry Kratafil, Jacksonville

America's
HOME COOKING

Risotto

DIRECTIONS

Make chicken broth, seasoning with onion powder, pepper and a little salt. Remove vegetables used to make broth when completed, leaving chicken chunks in broth. In a large pot, bring sauce to a boil, add beef and chicken chunks, and continue cooking. Pour rice into boiling sauce. Stir sauce constantly. While stirring, add broth 1 cup at a time. Continue this process for about 45 minutes or until all the broth is absorbed. Once broth is absorbed, stir in cheese. The risotto is done when it is smooth, not soupy. Serves 6. Serve hot with salad, fresh Italian bread and red wine.

INGREDIENTS

7 cups homemade chicken broth with chicken chunks

1 quart spaghetti sauce

1/2 pound ground beef

2 cups rice

1/2 cup grated romano cheese

SUBMITTED BY:
Joe LoBue, Adams Ridge

R.J.'s Mediterranean Dinner

DIRECTIONS

Position rack in middle of oven and preheat to 450 degrees. Season chicken thighs generously with salt and pepper. Heat large oven-proof skillet over medium-high heat. Add oil and heat until the oil shimmers. Cook chicken skin side down until golden and crispy, about 8 minutes. Do not move chicken while cooking. Turn chicken and brown for another 2 minutes. Transfer to a plate and tent with foil to keep warm. Pour off pan drippings, leaving enough oil in skillet to evenly cover the bottom, about 1 tablespoon. Add fennel, onions, garlic, oregano and red pepper flakes to skillet and cook until vegetables are just wilted, about 3 to 5 minutes. Stir in sun-dried tomatoes and olives. Arrange chicken, skin side up, on top of vegetable mixture and bake uncovered until chicken is cooked through, about 20 minutes.

INGREDIENTS

6 to 8 (2 1/2 to 3 pounds) bone-in chicken thighs with skin

Kosher salt and freshly ground black pepper, to taste

3 tablespoons extra virgin olive oil

1 medium bulb fennel, halved and cut into 1/2-inch wedges

1 medium red onion, sliced into 1/3- to 1/2-inch-thick wedges

4 to 6 cloves garlic, peeled and smashed

3/4 teaspoon dried oregano

1/4 teaspoon crushed red pepper flakes or to taste

1/2 cup roughly chopped oil-packed, sun-dried tomatoes

1/3 cup pitted kalamata olives

SUBMITTED BY:
R.J. Sule, Pittsburgh

Skillet Chicken and Bulgur

DIRECTIONS

Add enough olive oil to coat skillet and heat. While pan is heating, dice chicken. Add chicken to the pan when oil is hot. Add chopped vegetables and garlic to chicken. Sauté until chicken turns white and then add bulgur. Stir occasionally for 1 to 2 minutes. Add chicken stock to pan, season with salt and pepper, and add broccoli; stir. Bring pan to a boil, cover and simmer for about 30 minutes or until bulgur has absorbed stock. Serves 4 to 6.

INGREDIENTS

Olive oil

3 good-sized chicken breasts

3 stalks celery, chopped

3 carrots, coarsely chopped

1 small onion, diced

2 cloves garlic, minced

1 cup raw bulgur

2 1/2 cups chicken stock

Salt and pepper, to taste

1 (16-ounce) package frozen broccoli

SUBMITTED BY:
Charlie Hurka, Pittsburgh

Sunshine Chicken

DIRECTIONS

Combine curry powder, 1/2 teaspoon salt and pepper. Sprinkle seasonings over chicken and rub them into the top and bottom surfaces of each chicken piece; set aside. In a skillet, combine orange juice, water, brown sugar, mustard, 3/4 teaspoon salt and rice; mix well. Arrange chicken over rice. Bring skillet to a boil. Cover and simmer 20 minutes. Remove from heat and let stand, covered, until liquid is absorbed, about 5 minutes. Sprinkle with chopped parsley and serve.

INGREDIENTS

2 to 3 teaspoons curry powder

1 1/4 teaspoon salt

1/4 teaspoon pepper

6 whole, boneless chicken breasts, halved

1 1/2 cups orange juice

3/4 cups water

1 tablespoon brown sugar

1 teaspoon dry mustard

1 cup long-cooking rice

Parsley, for garnishing

SUBMITTED BY:
Kathy Martucci, Hampton

Teriyaki Chicken and Vegetable Stir-Fry

DIRECTIONS

In a large skillet, add all ingredients over medium heat. Cook and stir frequently for 20 minutes. Serve over long-grain and wild rice, if desired. Makes 2 servings.

INGREDIENTS

3 boneless, skinless chicken breasts, cut into small pieces

1/2 red onion, diced

3 plum tomatoes, diced

2 large mushrooms, diced

1/2 green pepper, diced

1/4 cup cooking oil

Salt, pepper and garlic salt, to taste

1/4 cup teriyaki sauce

SUBMITTED BY:
Jean Slesinger, Pittsburgh

Tomatoes and Chicken Skillet

DIRECTIONS

Heat dressing in a skillet over medium heat. Add chicken and garlic, cover and cook 5 minutes or until brown. Remove chicken and set aside. In the same skillet, add tomatoes and water. Stir in rice and bring to a boil. Reduce heat to low and simmer uncovered for 10 minutes. Return chicken to pan and sprinkle with cheese, tomato and cilantro. Serve warm.

INGREDIENTS

1/4 cup Italian dressing

4 boneless chicken breasts

2 cloves garlic

1 (28-ounce) can diced tomatoes

1 cup water

2 cups brown rice

1 cup shredded cheese, any kind

1 medium tomato, chopped

2 teaspoons chopped cilantro

SUBMITTED BY:
Joann Grosik, Mineral Point

America's
HOME COOKING

Unfried Chicken Fried Rice

DIRECTIONS

Heat oil in a skillet on medium-high heat. Add chicken; cook and stir 5 minutes or until cooked through. Add broth and soy sauce. Bring to a boil. Stir in vegetables and rice; cover. Reduce heat to low and cook 5 minutes. Stir before serving. Sprinkle with green onion, if desired. Serves 4 to 6.

INGREDIENTS

1 tablespoon vegetable oil

1 pound boneless, skinless chicken breasts, cut into bite-size pieces

1 (14 1/2-ounce) can chicken broth

4 teaspoons soy sauce

3 cups frozen stir-fry vegetables

2 cups uncooked instant white rice

1 green onion, sliced (optional)

SUBMITTED BY:
Lois Richardson, Springdale

One Skillet
Seafood

30-Minute Jambalaya 1-2-3

DIRECTIONS

Heat oil in a large skillet and stir-fry first 5 ingredients for about 6 minutes, adding additional oil as needed. Add tomatoes, garlic and herbs to skillet and simmer about 5 minutes. Prepare rice according to package directions and add to skillet. Stir gently to heat through. If desired, gently stir in 1 tablespoon hot sauce, salt and pepper. To serve, garnish with chopped scallions and offer additional hot sauce and cornbread on the side. Serves 8.

INGREDIENTS

1 (8-ounce) chicken breast, thinly sliced

8 ounces andouille sausage or skinless kielbasa, sliced into 1/2-inch pieces

1 pound frozen cooked shrimp, thawed

1 (16-ounce) bag frozen chopped onion and red and green peppers, thawed

1 stalk celery, finely diced

1 tablespoon olive oil

1 (28-ounce) can diced tomatoes with juice

2 teaspoons minced garlic

1/2 teaspoon dried thyme

1/2 teaspoon dried parsley

2 (8-ounce) bags microwave rice

1 tablespoon hot sauce (optional)

Salt and pepper, to taste

Chopped scallions, for garnishing

SUBMITTED BY:
Chris Bobick, Chalk Hill

Louisiana Shrimp

DIRECTIONS

Heat skillet and add oil and butter. Add garlic, shrimp and seasonings. Stir shrimp to coat and cook until slightly pink. Add enough wine to cover shrimp. Cover skillet and cook about 3 minutes. Serve hot with bread to dip in wine sauce.

INGREDIENTS

2 tablespoons oil

2 tablespoons butter

8 to 10 whole cloves garlic

2 to 3 pounds raw large shrimp in shell

2 crushed bay leaves

1 tablespoon Italian seasoning

1 tablespoon rosemary

1/2 to 1 (22 1/2-ounce) bottle white wine

Bread, for serving

SUBMITTED BY:
Arlene Miller, McMurray

America's
HOME COOKING

115

Mussels Marinara

DIRECTIONS

Heat oil in a Dutch oven over medium heat. Add onion and garlic; cook until light brown. Add tomatoes, oregano, red and black pepper, parsley and wine. Cook uncovered for about 15 minutes. Add mussels and cover skillet. Cook about 5 to 6 minutes, until mussels have opened. (Discard any unopened mussels.) Top with additional parsley and serve with crusty bread.

INGREDIENTS

3 tablespoons olive oil

1 small onion, chopped

4 cloves garlic, minced

1 (28-ounce) can crushed tomatoes

1/2 teaspoon oregano

Dash red pepper

Dash black pepper

1/2 cup chopped Italian parsley

1/2 cup white wine

2 pounds mussels in shells

Chopped Italian parsley, for garnishing

SUBMITTED BY:
Joseph Certo, Forest Hills

Paul's "AKA Curly" Rich Shrimp

DIRECTIONS

In a nonstick skillet, add butter, onion and garlic. Sauté gently until onions are translucent. Add alfredo sauce and 1/2 pound shredded mozzarella. Stir and add shrimp. Stir and sprinkle parsley on top. Add croutons to cover top of mixture. Gently press croutons into mixture. Sprinkle 1/2 pound mozzarella over croutons. Cover with lid and simmer for about 20 minutes.

INGREDIENTS

1/4 cup (1/2 stick) butter

1 large onion, chopped

1 large clove garlic, chopped

2 (16-ounce) jars alfredo sauce

1 pound shredded mozzarella cheese

1 pound of large or jumbo cleaned, raw shrimp

1/3 cup fresh diced parsley

2 tablespoons dried parsley

2 cups large unseasoned croutons

SUBMITTED BY:
Paul Cybulski, Clarksburg

Poblano Corn Chowder with Shrimp

DIRECTIONS

Blend 2 tablespoons butter and flour in a small bowl and set aside. Melt 2 tablespoons butter in a large pot over medium-high heat. Add onions, celery and chilies; sauté until soft, about 6 minutes. Add creamed corn and next 5 ingredients; bring to a boil. Reduce heat. Whisk in butter-flour mixture and simmer 15 minutes to blend flavors. Add shrimp and 4 tablespoons cilantro; simmer until shrimp are cooked through, about 5 additional minutes. Season with salt and pepper. Ladle chowder into bowls and sprinkle with remaining cilantro. Serves 6.

INGREDIENTS

4 tablespoons butter, at room temperature

2 tablespoons all-purpose flour

1 medium onion, finely chopped

3 celery stalks, finely chopped

2 large poblano chiles, seeded and chopped

2 (14 3/4-ounce to 15-ounce) cans cream-style corn

1 (16-ounce) package frozen corn kernels, thawed

2 (14-ounce) cans low-sodium chicken broth

1 cup whipping cream

2 teaspoons sugar

1/2 teaspoon cayenne pepper

1 pound uncooked shrimp, peeled, deveined and coarsely chopped

6 tablespoons chopped, fresh cilantro

SUBMITTED BY:
Kathy Geiger, Pittsburgh

Risotto with Shrimp, Fennel Seeds and Saffron

DIRECTIONS

Remove shells from shrimp and set shrimp aside in refrigerator. Put the shrimp shells in a small saucepan with 1 cup broth. Bring to a boil and simmer briskly until shells are pink, about 3 minutes. Remove and discard shells and set the broth aside. Heat butter and oil in a pressure cooker over medium-high heat until butter melts. Stir in onion and then rice. Continue stirring until rice becomes translucent, about 2 minutes. Stir in wine, then add the remaining 4 cups broth, fennel seeds, saffron, salt and reserved shrimp broth. Lock the pressure cooker lid and bring the pressure up over high heat, about 3 to 4 minutes. Reduce the heat to medium and cook for 5 minutes. Remove from heat and let sit 8 minutes to finish cooking. With the steam vent pointed away, gently release any remaining pressure. Remove the lid and stir in shrimp. Put the lid back on without locking it and let sit 4 minutes. Stir in cheese and parsley; serve immediately. Serves 4.

INGREDIENTS

1 pound medium shrimp, deveined

5 cups chicken broth

2 tablespoons butter

1 tablespoon olive oil

1/4 cup finely chopped yellow onion

1 1/2 cups arborio rice

1/2 cup white wine

1/2 teaspoon fennel seeds

Large pinch saffron threads

1/2 teaspoon salt

1/3 cup freshly grated romano cheese

2 tablespoons fresh flat-leaf parsley

SUBMITTED BY:

Joseph Certo, Forest Hills

Seafood Pasta with Sun-Dried Tomatoes and Lemon

DIRECTIONS

Cook pasta in a large amount of boiling salted water until quite firm. Drain pasta and set aside. Place olive oil and butter in a large skillet over low heat. Add garlic and sauté for a few seconds. Increase heat to medium-high, add shrimp and scallops to skillet and sauté until shrimp just turn pink. Add stock or clam juice and pasta to skillet. Increase heat to high. Cook until most of the liquid has been absorbed, stirring occasionally. Add tomatoes, parsley and lemon zest, tossing to combine. Season with salt and pepper and serve immediately.

INGREDIENTS

8 ounces pasta

2 tablespoons olive oil

2 tablespoons unsalted butter

2 to 3 cloves garlic, minced

1/2 pound uncooked medium shrimp, peeled

1/2 pound sea scallops

1/2 cup fish stock or clam juice

1/4 cup sun-dried tomatoes, diced

1/4 cup parsley, chopped

1 lemon, for zest

Salt and pepper, to taste

SUBMITTED BY:
Jim Baran, Pittsburgh

America's HOME COOKING

Tuna Pilaf

DIRECTIONS

In a large, heavy skillet, cook and stir onion and celery in hot oil until onion is tender. Add vegetables and water; heat to just boiling. Cover and simmer 10 minutes or until vegetables are tender. Add remaining ingredients, stir gently until well mixed and heated through. Serves 6 to 8.

INGREDIENTS

1 small onion, thinly sliced

1/2 cup diagonally sliced celery

1 tablespoon oil

1 (10-ounce) package frozen mixed vegetables

1/2 cup water

3 cups unsalted cooked rice

2 (6 1/2-ounce) cans tuna

1 (8-ounce) can water chestnuts, drained and sliced thin

1/4 cup soy sauce

SUBMITTED BY:
Theresa Gawryk, Pittsburgh

America's
HOME COOKING

Pasta

Easy Linguine Toss

DIRECTIONS

In a small bowl, mix together all ingredients except pasta. Cook pasta and drain when tender. Put pasta back in pot and mix quickly with tomato mixture-mix as quickly as possible while the pasta is as hot as possible. Replace lid and keep warm until ready to serve. Serve with a salad and Italian rolls or bread.

INGREDIENTS

1 (6-ounce) can tomato paste

3/4 cup extra-virgin olive oil

1 cup grated parmesan or romano cheese

1/4 cup finely minced, chopped onion

2 teaspoons minced garlic

3 tablespoons chopped, fresh flat-leaf parsley

1 teaspoon brown sugar or 1 packet sugar substitute

Salt and pepper, to taste

1 teaspoon Italian seasonings

1 pound whole wheat or enriched linguine or spaghetti

SUBMITTED BY:
Rosemarie Weleski, Natrona Heights

One-Pot Pesto Pasta

DIRECTIONS

In a large saucepan, cook sausage or ground beef until no longer pink, stirring occasionally. Drain fat; stir in broth. Bring to a boil and gradually add spaghetti. Reduce heat and simmer covered, stirring occasionally, for 25 minutes or until spaghetti is tender and most of the liquid is absorbed. Remove from heat; stir in pesto. Transfer to a serving dish and sprinkle with cheese. Serve with salad and garlic bread. Serves 4.

INGREDIENTS

1 pound bulk Italian sausage or ground beef

3 cups reduced-sodium chicken broth

8 ounces spaghetti, broken

3 to 5 tablespoons pesto

1/4 cup shredded parmesan cheese

SUBMITTED BY:
Ashlea Hilliard, Columbus

America's
HOME COOKING

One-Skillet Recipe

DIRECTIONS

In a large skillet, cook chicken with garlic in vegetable oil until chicken is no longer pink. Add pasta side dish to skillet according to package directions. Cook for 4 to 5 minutes. Add frozen peas or other vegetable. Turn heat to low and cook, covered, for 5 minutes. Add canned vegetables last; stir. Season dish with salt, pepper, parsley, oregano and basil, to taste. Cook 1 to 2 more minutes. Turn off heat; let dish sit for a few minutes with the lid on. Sprinkle with romano cheese and serve. Serves 5.

INGREDIENTS

1 to 2 chicken breasts, cut into bite-size pieces, or 2 to 3 cups leftover chicken

2 cloves, garlic, chopped

2 tablespoons vegetable oil

1 (5-ounce) box angel hair pasta and sauce side dish

1 to 2 cups of peas, corn or any other frozen or fresh vegetable

Salt and pepper, to taste

Parsley, to taste

Oregano, to taste

Basil, to taste

1 (15-ounce) can spinach and juice

2 (15-ounce) cans navy beans and juice

1/2 cup romano cheese

SUBMITTED BY:
Melissa Kiehl, St. Malachy's

Pasta Gianni

DIRECTIONS

Preheat oven to 350 degrees. On stovetop, brown sausage, onions and mushrooms in an oven-safe casserole. When brown, drain excess fat and return to stovetop. Add tomatoes, tomato puree and evaporated milk. Mix well and heat through. When hot, add cheese mix and cooked pasta; mix well. Sprinkle dish with grated romano cheese and bake, uncovered, until hot and bubbly.

INGREDIENTS

1 pound loose hot, mild or mixed Italian sausage

1 medium onion, chopped

1 pound fresh mushrooms, quartered

1 (16-ounce) can diced tomatoes with basil, garlic and oregano

1 (10 3/4-ounce) can tomato puree

1 (12-ounce) can fat-free evaporated milk

1 (8-ounce) package shredded Italian cheese mix

1 pound (or more) cooked pasta

1/4 to 1/2 cup grated fresh romano cheese

SUBMITTED BY:
Stephanie Matiak, Pittsburgh

Skillet Lasagna

DIRECTIONS

Cook noodles for 8 minutes or according to package directions; drain. In a small bowl, mix cottage cheese and spinach. Spread 1 cup meat sauce over the bottom of a skillet. Layer a third of the noodles over sauce. Spoon half of the remaining sauce over the noodles. Add Italian seasonings, to taste. Top with another third of the noodles and spread cottage cheese over them. Sprinkle half the pizza cheese over the cottage cheese layer. Top with remaining noodles and sauce. Cover. Bring to rapid, hard simmer over high heat. Reduce heat to medium and simmer 10 minutes. Sprinkle remaining pizza cheese blend and grated parmesan cheese on top. Cover and simmer 2 minutes. Remove from heat and let stand 10 minutes.

INGREDIENTS

1/2 pound wide egg noodles or spirals

1 pound cottage cheese

1 (10-ounce) package frozen creamed or plain spinach, thawed and drained

1 (32-ounce) jar meat sauce

Oregano, to taste

Parsley, to taste

Basil, to taste

1 (8-ounce) package shredded pizza cheese

1/4 cup grated parmesan cheese

SUBMITTED BY:
Mary Lee Gannon, O'Hara Township

Skillet Pierogie Supper

DIRECTIONS

Melt butter in a large skillet over medium heat. When butter foam subsides, place pierogies in skillet, flat side down, in a single layer. Season with salt and pepper; let cook until golden brown on the bottom. Turn pierogies over and layer the green beans and onion; season again with salt and pepper. Cover, reduce heat to medium low and steam for about 15 minutes, gently tossing all ingredients together about every 5 minutes. If skillet seems to be drying out too fast, add a little more butter or 1 tablespoon water. When beans and onions are just about tender, add ham and toss to incorporate. Cover and cook another 2 to 3 minutes or until vegetables are tender and ham is warmed through.

INGREDIENTS

1/4 cup (1/2 stick) butter

1 dozen pierogies, thawed quickly in warm water and drained, if frozen

Salt and freshly ground black pepper, to taste

1 pound fresh green beans, trimmed

1 large vidalia onion, cut into large chunks and then separated

2 cups cubed leftover ham or 1 ham slice

SUBMITTED BY:
Erin DeCaro, Hempfield Township

Spaghetti in a Skillet

DIRECTIONS

Season ground meat and onions with salt and pepper, to taste, and cook in a large nonstick skillet. Drain off most of the fat. Break spaghetti in half and layer over meat and onion mixture. Pour tomato sauce into skillet. Cover and cook approximately 45 minutes over low to medium heat, stirring occasionally. The dish is done when the spaghetti has absorbed nearly all the tomato sauce. Serves 4.

VARATION

Add any the following: Italian seasoning, fresh sliced mushrooms (during the last 10 minutes of cooking), mini frozen meatballs or tomato juice instead of tomato sauce.

INGREDIENTS

1 pound ground meat

1 large or 2 small onions, cut in 8 pieces

Salt and pepper, to taste

1 (8-ounce) box uncooked thin spaghetti

1 (46-ounce) can tomato sauce

SUBMITTED BY:
Joan Hudson, North Huntingdon

Spaghettini alle Vongole in Padella

DIRECTIONS

Add the first 4 ingredients to a large skillet over medium heat. (The anchovies will dissolve.) Add clam juice and wine. Bring to a gentle bubble. Add chicken broth and bring to a boil. Add spaghettini, covering pasta with the liquid. Once pasta is softened, stir, making sure it doesn't stick. Cook about 15 to 20 minutes, until pasta absorbs the broth and becomes al dente. When 1/2 of the liquid is absorbed, add baby clams. Additional broth may be added near the end of the cooking time to insure the pasta is creamy. Sprinkle with parsley and serve immediately.

INGREDIENTS

2 cloves garlic, crushed and minced

3 tablespoons extra-virgin olive oil

5 anchovies, chopped (optional)

1 teaspoon hot pepper flakes (optional)

1 (10-ounce) can whole baby clams, drained, reserving juice

1 cup white wine

1 to 1 1/2 quarts chicken broth

1 pound spaghettini

Chopped parsley, for garnishing

SUBMITTED BY:
Denise Catalfamo, Pittsburgh

HOME COOKING

131

Vegetables

Asparagus, Pancetta and Toasted Pignoli Nuts

DIRECTIONS

Cook asparagus in a steaming rack or microwave 3 to 4 minutes until crisp-tender. In a large sauté pan, place diced pancetta and cook until brown. Add onion and cook 2 to 3 minutes. Add minced garlic and sauté 1 minute. Add heavy cream and bring to a boil. Add romano cheese. Toss with hot pasta. Top with pignoli nuts and additional romano cheese.

INGREDIENTS

1 pound asparagus, trimmed, rinsed and cut into 1-inch diagonals

4 ounces pancetta, diced

1/2 cup chopped onion

1 clove garlic, minced

1 cup heavy cream

1/4 cup grated romano cheese

2 tablespoons pignoli nuts, stirred in hot skillet until toasted

SUBMITTED BY:
Joseph Certo, Forest Hills

Garlic Broccoli

DIRECTIONS

Cook garlic in olive oil in a large nonstick skillet over medium-high heat, stirring constantly until tender. Add broccoli and next 4 ingredients; cover and cook 5 minutes or until crisp-tender. Sprinkle with parmesan cheese. Serves 4.

INGREDIENTS

1 clove garlic, minced

3/4 teaspoon olive oil

2 cups fresh broccoli florets

2 tablespoons sliced green onions

1/4 cup chicken broth

1/8 teaspoon salt

1/8 teaspoon pepper

2 tablespoons grated parmesan cheese

SUBMITTED BY:
Kathy Geiger, Pittsburgh

America's
HOME COOKING

Potato Pepperoni Supper

DIRECTIONS

Scrub potatoes, leaving skins on. Using a food processor, mandolin or sharp knife, slice potatoes about 1/4 inch thick. In a large nonstick skillet, melt butter over medium heat. Place potatoes in skillet, starting in the center, work out in a circle and overlap potatoes to cover the bottom of the skillet and halfway up the sides. Toss the chopped onions on the potatoes and season with salt and pepper. Cover skillet and reduce heat to medium-low. Cook for 20 minutes, or until potatoes are tender and nicely brown on the bottom. Pour tomato sauce evenly over potatoes and add sliced pepperoni and cheese as if making a pizza. Cover and continue to cook over low until cheese melts, about 10 minutes. Slice and serve while very hot.

INGREDIENTS

4 medium red-skinned potatoes

1 tablespoon butter or margarine

1/2 small onion, diced

1/4 teaspoon salt

1/4 teaspoon pepper

1 (8-ounce) can tomato sauce

4 ounces sliced pepperoni

1 cup shredded cheese

SUBMITTED BY:
Kimberlee Love, North Side

Succotash

DIRECTIONS

Fry bacon in skillet. Remove bacon, leaving grease in pan. Sauté squash, okra, beans, onions and peppers until soft. Add corn, tomatoes, parsley and seasonings. Cut bacon into small pieces and add to vegetables.

INGREDIENTS

6 strips bacon

1 cup diced yellow squash

1 cup fresh or frozen okra

1 cup lima beans

1 small onion, diced

1/2 green pepper, diced

1/2 red pepper, diced

1 cup canned corn

1 tomato, diced

1/2 cup chopped fresh parsley

Garlic powder, to taste

Salt and pepper, to taste

SUBMITTED BY:
Nancy Polinsky, Squirrel Hill

America's
HOME COOKING

Desserts

Apple Skillet Cobbler

DIRECTIONS

Preheat oven to 350 degrees. Heat sugar and butter in a 10-inch skillet over medium heat. Add apples and continue cooking until the sugar melts and forms an amber-colored syrup. Combine the baking mix with 1/4 cup sugar and grated cheese. Add enough milk to form a soft dough. Spoon over apple mixture and bake for 20 minutes or until top is lightly browned.

INGREDIENTS

1 cup sugar

4 tablespoons butter

6 apples, peeled, cored and diced

1 1/2 cups buttermilk baking mix

1/4 cup sugar

1 cup grated sharp cheddar cheese

3/4 to 1 cup milk

SUBMITTED BY:
Chris Fennimore, Pittsburgh

Skillet Cherry Cobbler

Directions

In a small bowl, combine baking mix, sugar and orange peel. Stir in milk, 1 tablespoon at a time and combine until just moistened. Set aside. In a nonstick skillet, combine pie filling and orange juice; bring to a boil, stirring occasionally. Drop biscuit mixture in mounds onto boiling cherry mixture. Reduce heat; cover and simmer for 10 minutes. Uncover; simmer 5 to 7 minutes longer or until toothpick inserted into a dumpling comes out clean. Serves 4 to 5.

Ingredients

1 cup baking mix

1 tablespoon sugar

1 to 1 1/2 teaspoons grated orange peel

4 tablespoons milk

1 (21-ounce) can cherry or other flavor pie filling

1/2 cup orange juice

Submitted by:

Terry Kratafil, Jacksonville

America's
HOME COOKING

Tropical Trifle

DIRECTIONS

Tear or cut cake into bite-size pieces. Prepare pudding according to package directions. In a trifle dish, layer ingredients in the following order: 1/2 the cake pieces, canned crushed pineapple, 1/2 the cake pieces, vanilla pudding, sliced bananas and cherry pie filling. Finish with whipped topping.

INGREDIENTS

1 angel food cake

1 (3-ounce) box vanilla pudding

1 (20-ounce) can crushed pineapple

Sliced bananas

1 (21-ounce) can cherry pie filling

1 (8-ounce) container whipped topping

SUBMITTED BY:
Ruth Deighan, Brookline

Index

Recipes were prepared on "America's Home Cooking: One Skillet"

Index

Recipes were prepared on "America's Home Cooking: One Skillet"

Index

Recipes were prepared on "America's Home Cooking: One Skillet"

Index

Recipes were prepared on "America's Home Cooking: One Skillet"

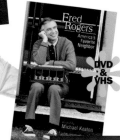

ISBN 0-9769936-6-X

51495

9 780976 993667

AMERICA'S HOME COOKING / ONE SKILLET